# Delta Rainbow

To Stephanie and
Reynolds,
Thanks for all you
have done for so
many!! Fondly,
Jean

Oh, Steph and marvelous
Reynolds,
Two amazing
people who (know)
the strength of Betty
love,
Sally

# Delta Rainbow

## The Irrepressible Betty Bobo Pearson

Sally Palmer Thomason

*with Jean Carter Fisher*

University Press of Mississippi / Jackson

Willie Morris Books in Memoir and Biography

www.upress.state.ms.us

The University Press of Mississippi is a member
of the Association of American University Presses.

Photographs are from the collection of Betty Bobo Pearson.

Library of Congress Cataloging-in-Publication Data
Names: Thomason, Sally Palmer, 1934– | Fisher, Jean Carter.
Title: Delta rainbow : the irrepressible Betty Bobo Pearson / Sally Palmer
    Thomason with Jean Carter Fisher.
Description: Jackson : University Press of Mississippi, 2016. | Series:
    Willie Morris books in memoir and biography | Includes bibliographical
    references and index.
Identifiers: LCCN 2015044919 (print) | LCCN 2016010581 (ebook) | ISBN
    9781496806642 (hardback) | ISBN 9781496806659 (epub single) | ISBN
    9781496806666 (epub institutional) | ISBN 9781496806673 (pdf single) |
    ISBN 9781496806680 (pdf institutional)
Subjects: LCSH: Pearson, Betty Bobo, 1922– | Women civil rights
    workers—Mississippi—Biography. | Civil rights
    workers—Mississippi—Biography. | Women, White—Mississippi—Biography. |
    Women marines—United States—Biography. | United States. Marine
    Corps—Biography. | Women plantation owners—Mississippi—Delta
    (Region)—Biography. | Delta (Miss. : Region)—Biography. | Civil rights
    movements—Mississippi—History—20th century. | Mississippi—Race
    relations—History—20th century. | BISAC: BIOGRAPHY & AUTOBIOGRAPHY /
    Women. | HISTORY / United States / State & Local / South (AL, AR, FL, GA,
    KY, LA, MS, NC, SC, TN, VA, WV). | SOCIAL SCIENCE / Discrimination & Race
    Relations.
Classification: LCC F345.3.P43 T47 2016 (print) | LCC F345.3.P43 (ebook) |
    DDC 323.092—dc23

LC record available at http://lccn.loc.gov/2015044919

Dedicated to the memory of John T. Fisher,
a white man with a heart of many colors. . . .

*There is a concept in Judaism that there are six righteous people on earth at one time. Betty Pearson is one of them. She is my hero . . . a moral compass. She is transparent . . . straightforward, and such a respectful listener.*

—Dr. Susan M. Glisson, Executive Director, William Winter Institute for Racial Reconciliation, University of Mississippi

# Contents

# Preface

Betty Bobo Pearson's roots reach deep into the soil of the Mississippi Delta. A seventh-generation, plantation-born Southerner, she grew up in her namesake town, Bobo, and in Clarksdale. Despite the economic challenges during the Great Depression, land and family assured her a secure position in her world. Life was good. However, after she and Bill Pearson married in 1947, the world of Betty's childhood began to fracture, revealing disturbing realities. Betty and Bill's basic beliefs about race were fundamentally at odds with those of Betty's family and most of her friends. These differences resulted in great anguish for Betty.

During the Emmett Till trial in Sumner, Mississippi, which took place in 1955 when Betty was a young wife and mother, the majority of white Mississippians resented the worldwide publicity focused on their home state. After the initial shock accompanying discovery of Till's mutilated body, almost everyone Betty knew refused to talk about the murder and the trial. Betty, however, was determined to learn all she could about the tragedy, and she managed to obtain a press pass to the trial. She and her friend Florence Mars were the only white women permitted in the press section of the courtroom. What they witnessed changed Betty's life.

Her story, gathered from in-depth conversations with Betty herself, her husband Bill, her daughter Erie, and many friends and colleagues, is the story of a fiercely independent woman in what was then a very paternalistic society. She is a woman who makes up her mind and acts in accordance with what she believes is right and with a transparency that clearly displays her values. Betty Bobo Pearson was one of the most outspoken leaders of the civil rights movement in a culturally and racially divided Mississippi. Yet if you check the invitation list of every prominent wedding, garden party, country club soiree, and social function in the Mississippi Delta from the late 1940s until the early 2000s, you will find the names of Mr. and Mrs. William Pearson.

Betty's life is a multi-faceted prism that throws light in many different directions. As a dynamic leader, amazing counselor, fabulous hostess, master gardener, and treasured friend, she is seen by many as a compassionate, but hard-headed hero. Betty seems inherently to know how to use her wit, her charm, her intelligence, her social position, her connections, and her stubbornness to get what she wants. Yet she is a woman who, when troubled, is not afraid to confront her own demons.

Having celebrated her ninety-third birthday in 2015, Betty looks back and remembers, "That whole era of resistance was terrible because I was so torn between what I had to do and my relationship with my parents . . . my family. It was very painful for me. And then, I just got disgusted, because I just felt, and still feel like folks of our generation should decide what's right and do it, regardless of what other people think." The following pages are not a documented history of an era. They are, rather, a word portrait written to try to capture the complete picture—the ups and downs in the life of a remarkable woman who made a significant difference in the lives of many.

I first met Betty Pearson on a sunny, late September morning at her daughter's house in Davis, California, about three years ago. We exchanged greetings in the front hall and proceeded into the living room for the interview. After casual chat about my delayed flight and late arrival the night before, I excused myself to go to the bedroom for my tape recorder. On my return to the living room I found it empty. No Betty. Wandering around the house, I glanced out a window, and there she was, bending over stiff legged, pulling up weeds. It was a scene that I soon realized served as an apt metaphor for Betty Bobo Pearson's life. When I went out to join her, she said, "I've got to pull out these weeds . . . doesn't matter if I get my hands dirty. . . . I like things right—neat and clean. I love doing it."

What in Betty's makeup or her experience made her become a civic beacon? What in her character made Betty choose the struggle, the pain? Close friends and colleagues tell stories about Betty's role as a take-charge organizer impatient for things to be done "correctly," one who occasionally displayed a bit of temper. But there are more tales of a fun-loving, smart, inquisitive, active adventurer, who is also an empathetic listener when personal problems are shared.

A multi-faceted woman, Betty Bobo Pearson has many character traits. And it is those traits that have led, fed, and sustained her through her remarkable life. It is those traits that provide the backbone of the following story.

# Delta Rainbow

# *Prologue*

---

*You are here for a purpose.*
—Elizabeth Brock Bobo

When she was older Betty had no personal memory of the accident, only the details her relatives related in later years. But the accident's impact on her life, on her character, on the woman she became is undeniable.

## October 1923

Exhausted after spending seven hours behind the wheel driving on largely gravel roads, Lenora Bobo caught sight of smoke puffs coming from a locomotive snaking through a distant cotton field. Impatient to get home, she figured she could beat the train and pressed her foot hard on the accelerator. The car hit a huge bump, causing her father-in-law—sleeping on the seat beside her—to lunge forward, almost hitting his head on the windshield. They would never make it. Silently cursing her luck, Lenora pulled to a stop beside the railroad tracks on the outskirts of Glendora, a small town about forty miles south of Bobo and home.

The next ten minutes seemed like ten hours, as Lenora's meticulously manicured fingernails drummed the steering wheel, matching their rhythm with the train's clacking over jointed track. The 1922 Chevrolet touring car she drove looked like an enormous, black bathtub, with a wide running board along each side, genuine leather upholstered seats, and four rubber tires wrapped around spoked wooden wheels. Her father-in-law, Fincher Bobo, again dozed on the front seat beside Lenora. Betty, her eighteen-month-old daughter, having wriggled off her Grandmother Bessie's lap, stood on the back seat next to the door, wanting to get a better look at the huge, noisy monster lumbering past.

Before the family left Gulf Shores that morning, Fincher had unsnapped the Chevy's isinglass curtains and rolled them up tight. The wide-open top half of the car, with its canvas roof, gave the family a better view—plus a brisk breeze when they were under way. Now stopped at the railroad crossing only half an hour from home, they sat in the late afternoon calm. Cotton fields, picked clean, stretched out on both sides of the road. Dusty ditches indicated that it had been weeks since the last rain, but the late October air held the first nip of fall. Lenora was eager to see her husband, Bob, who stayed home to finish getting in the crop. The trip to visit her sister Erie on the gulf was an impromptu mini-vacation, designed to help Fincher, Bob's father, recover from his recent stroke.

Passage of the afternoon train through the little hamlet of Glendora, Mississippi, was the big event of the day for the small passel of young boys assembled at the crossing. That afternoon, the fancy car stopped at the crossing was an added attraction. Lenora, a pretty, dark-haired, young matron fond of children, would normally joke with the youngsters and enjoy their attention, but today she took no notice of them. Her patience was at an end as she reached back over her seat to pull Betty away from the large opening above the back door.

The last freight car finally passed, and a crewman, standing on the caboose's rear platform, waved for Lenora to drive on across. She only got midway. A second train, hidden from view by the passing train, hurtled full speed from the other direction and crashed into the car on the passenger side.

Little Betty flew out onto the cowcatcher attached to the front of the oncoming train's engine. Betty's grandmother, severely injured, lay unconscious on the backseat. In the front seat, Lenora, four months pregnant, sat rigid, in shock, gripping the steering wheel. Betty's grandfather, killed instantly by the impact, lay dead on the seat beside Lenora.

As the train hissed to a stop, one of the young boys who witnessed the devastating crash saw a small body roll off the front of the engine into a ditch a few hundred feet away. He ran to pick up the crying toddler and carried her back to the lady in the driver's seat who screamed hysterically. "My baby, where is my baby?"

On hearing crashing steel and screeching brakes, horrified townspeople streamed from their houses to gawk at the brutally injured, bleeding occupants of the now demolished touring car. The uniformed conductor stepped off the train to take control of the situation. He ordered people to stand back, as Fincher Bobo's body was lifted onto the northbound train. The conductor told two black porters to carry Betty's grandmother, moaning with pain, into one of the empty double seats in a passenger car, where, supported by pillows, she could recline. The conductor then lifted little Betty out of her mother's arms before assisting Lenora, who was barely able to walk, up the steps into the same car. He gently placed the whimpering child back in her mother's arms for the thirty-mile trip to Clarksdale.

It isn't hard to imagine Bob Bobo's heavy heart when the train pulled into Clarksdale and he unloaded his emotionally devastated wife, his crying child, and his father's body. Bob's severely injured mother remained on the train to be taken to a hospital in Memphis. The town's undertaker loaded Fincher's body into the back of his truck, and Bobo relatives stepped forward to care for Betty and Lenora. As the train began to pull out of the station, Bob hastily boarded to take his mother, now conscious and in terrible pain, to the Campbell Clinic in Memphis, where she would stay for over two months while her broken pelvis mended. On that fateful day, Robert E. Bobo III, whom everyone called Bob, took charge of a substantial part of the Bobo family's holdings. He was twenty-one years old.

That night Betty and her mother did not go home to Bobo, the small town eight and a half miles south of Clarksdale. Instead, they stayed with family in Clarksdale. Stunned by grief and shock, Lenora was inconsolable. Little Betty would not stop crying. Bob's cousin, Robbie, with whom Lenora and Betty were staying, suspected that the child might also be injured—especially when she continued to cry through the night and into the next morning. A doctor was needed. In 1923, the only x-ray machine in Clarksdale belonged to the dentist on Main Street. Robbie phoned the dentist, and Betty was carried to his office where tiny pictures, one after another, were taken of her entire body. The x-rays revealed a broken collarbone on one side and on the other a broken arm. Betty's father arrived back in Clarksdale, staying only a few hours before turning right around. He once again boarded the train to Memphis, this time accompanied by Lenora and little Betty. At the Campbell Clinic, the child was put in a body cast, with her arms extended over her head. Although her activities were severely restricted, Betty remembers nothing of that time—neither how long she was in Memphis, nor how long she was in the cast. But she knows that she had been home for at least a month or two before her grandmother returned to Bobo.

Four generations lived under one roof in the big house in Bobo. Sitting at the edge of acres of cotton fields, it was a large, two-story clapboard structure with wide porches, surrounded by huge oaks. The whistle-stop for Bobo, plus several small shanties, stood close by across a dirt road. Betty, her parents, and little Bob (after he was born the following March, unharmed by the accident) lived upstairs on one side of the house. Betty's grandmother's parents, the Brocks, lived in another upstairs suite. Bessie's bed and bathroom, which she had shared with her husband before the accident, were downstairs. When she was in the hospital, she could not grasp that Fincher was dead, but when she came home to Bobo, she fell to pieces. Utterly alone, grieving for her husband, she begged Betty's parents to let the little girl come down and stay with her. Betty's bed went downstairs; it would be years before it left her grandmother's room.

During those years, Bessie put Betty to bed every night and told her a story. Often she spoke about the train wreck from which Betty was miraculously saved, but sometimes she related a tale from her childhood on a farm near Aberdeen, North Carolina, or reminisced about the time she first met Betty's grandfather Fincher. After the bedtime story, Bessie listened to Betty's prayers and tucked her in between soft, lavender-scented linen sheets. Every night before turning out the light, she said, "Betty, God reached down and plucked you from in front of that train because He has something very special he wants you to do with your life."

# The Trial

*The Emmett Till murder was the first great media event of the civil rights movement.*
　—David Halberstam

*This is a time when the world is in need of a prayer.*
　—President Dwight D. Eisenhower

**September 1955**

It had been three weeks since the discovery of Emmett Till's horrifically mutilated body, which had been beaten, shot in the head, and sunk in the Tallahatchie River, a cotton gin fan tied around his neck with barbed wire. When Till's body was sent back to his mother in Chicago, she insisted on an open casket and a public funeral. Mamie Till Bradley wanted the world to see what had happened to her young son. Thousands upon thousands of Negroes flocked into a downtown funeral home to view the unrecognizable remains of the fourteen-year-old black boy from Chicago who had been visiting his great uncle in Money, Mississippi. The boy, who allegedly had whistled at a white woman, was murdered in Mississippi by Mississippians. Grotesque pictures of his featureless remains, splashed across the front pages of the nation's newspapers, confirmed an act of unquestionable savagery. Two white men, half-brothers J. W. Milam and Roy Bryant, were arrested and indicted for the kidnapping and murder of Emmett Till.

The world was aghast. In Sumner, Mississippi, the initial shock and public horror over the brutality of the murder was palpable. But Betty Pearson, a scion of one the first white families of the Mississippi Delta, and at age thirty-three mistress of Rainbow Plantation, four miles south of Sumner, found one thing strange. After the first few days, no one in town would talk about the murder or the upcoming trial. A curtain of silence fell. Most everyone she knew felt resentful about the incredible amount of international attention and vindictive spotlight trained on their little town. An aggrieved undercurrent arose from a general sentiment that the whole procedure was unfair. After all, the murder took place in Leflore, not Tallahatchie County, and the body was found not in their county, but in the river between the two counties. The trial, set in the Tallahatchie County Courthouse, marked Sumner with undeserved notoriety—or at least profound embarrassment. One of Betty's younger friends, who was serving in the military at Fort Chaffey, Arkansas, during that time, admitted when anyone asked him where he was from, he said, "a little bit south of Memphis," never mentioning Sumner because it was being denigrated by every newspaper in the country.

The trial for the murder of Emmett Till began on Monday, September 19, 1955. On that morning, Betty flashed the press pass she had borrowed from her husband's uncle, the editor of the local newspaper, and pulled into a restricted parking spot behind the courthouse. Though it was still early in the day, the sweltering heat was intensified by the large crowd—easily numbering over a hundred, more than a sixth of Sumner's total population—seeking entrance. She later learned that two hundred and eighty persons, both black and white, had packed into the courtroom to witness the proceedings. The crowd that gathered in Court Square and along Court Street reached all the way to Cassidy Bayou, a block away.

Most of Betty's friends in Sumner lived in one of the stately mansions or fine homes along that bayou's dark, still waters lined with ancient cypress trees—the "socially correct" part of town. Harvey Henderson, a lawyer in Sumner, who was like part of the Pearson family—a childhood friend of her husband who'd been best man in their wedding nine years earlier—lived in the house two doors down from the Court Street bridge. Harvey had represented J. W. Milam on a civil matter, and when Milam and Roy Bryant were indicted for kidnapping Emmett Till, they'd gone to see Harvey. He told the two accused men he did not handle criminal cases, but would help, and he referred them to his law partner, Sidney Carlton.

What happened next still made Betty angry sixty years later. There were five lawyers in Sumner in 1955, and they all agreed to be advocates for Milam and Bryant. She couldn't believe it. These were some of her best friends, people she'd known all of her life. Betty felt every lawyer in the county (there were only white lawyers at that time) colluded, banding together to defend Milam and Bryant. She understood the American legal system guarantees anyone accused of a crime the right to legal representation—but not from every lawyer in the county. That fact made it seem as if all white people in Mississippi defended the murderers.

Headlines like "Barbaric" and "The Lynching State" followed the indictment. But not every white person in the state fell under such rubrics. Betty knew how she felt and how Bill felt. She knew there were other fair-minded people in Mississippi. What could she do? How could her voice be heard? She had to see the trial for herself and hear what those lawyers had to say. She had to meet and talk to some of the reporters from around the country to let them know not all Mississippians were monsters. Reporters from every major city in the South, as well as from some European and many national publications—including the *Times* (London), the *New York Times*, the *Detroit Free Press*, *Time* magazine, and *Life* magazine—flooded into town over the weekend. But everyone Betty knew in Sumner, except those directly involved with the trial, stayed home behind drawn curtains.

Betty Pearson had never before attended a trial. In 1955, the courtroom was an all-male domain. White women could vote, but by law they were excluded from jury duty. (No blacks served on juries, although 4.3 per cent of the Negro population was registered to vote.) As she parked the car, Betty was relieved that Bill's uncle had given her two press passes, one for her and one for Florence "Flossie" Mars, guaranteeing not only a place to park, but also seats at the press table inside. Flossie, Betty's best friend from college days, had come up from Philadelphia, Mississippi, where she lived, a hundred miles south of Sumner. The two friends had talked on the phone every day since news of the murder broke. Flossie shared Betty's outrage. As they were about to enter the back door of the courthouse, the entrance for the press, Harry Dogan, an old family friend and the ex-sheriff of Tallahatchie County, stopped Betty. His worn face under the ubiquitous panama hat, which all Southern men wore in hot weather, looked troubled. White males in this patriarchal Southern society felt the need to protect the sensibilities of white women. "Betty," he said, "you shouldn't be going to this trial. You will be hearing things that no white lady should hear." Thanking Mr. Dogan for his concern, Betty pushed open the door and entered the large, imposing brick building, which, until that moment, had been a mere backdrop to her life. Walking into the Tallahatchie County Courthouse on that historic day in 1955, Betty Bobo Pearson had her eyes blasted open.

Betty grew up in a segregated society and understood how racist it was, but her family, her friends, everyone she knew, treated Negroes with decency, and often with true affection. Theirs was a paternalistic racism, a belief she felt was misguided, but never violent, never vicious. Her father would never harm, much less kill, a Negro. She knew her father, her moral beacon in most areas, thought skin color made a difference. When, as a college student, she began to find her voice, Betty and her father often argued about the ethical implications of segregation. Her father believed it was his duty to take care of Negroes, who were good people, but an inferior race. Betty argued vehemently that the color of one's skin made no difference. A person should be judged on his or her merits, values, and behavior. She believed black people were different because they did not have access to equal education. Yet, for years her sentiments were only theoretical. Beyond the occasional arguments with her father and heated discussions in her philosophy class as a senior at Ole Miss, she thought little about racial issues or the plight of the Negro.

Now, looking at the faces of the white people in that courtroom, Betty realized for the first time in her life how deep set their feelings were. She saw pure hatred. Who were these people? They were neighbors, citizens of the surrounding counties: Tallahatchie, Coahoma, Leflore, Sunflower. They were farmers, laborers, merchants, tradesmen, and their women. They were people she'd lived with all her life. Yet, Betty realized, she never before had grasped the raw hostility these people harbored. Who were they? They were from a different world—Milam and Bryant's world. A world of mistrust, violence, and hatred toward Negroes. A world very different from her own.

Never before had she clearly understood how her privileged heritage protected her. For the first time in her thirty-three years, the quiet security of Betty's Delta world was shaken. She saw beyond the façade of sensibility and decency she'd known all of her life. Walking into that courtroom on that hot September morning had thrown into sharp relief the unspoken and largely unacknowledged class structure of society in the Delta—Betty Pearson's society. In addition to the sharp divide between blacks and whites, there were two classes in the white community: the land owners and professionals, who belonged to the country clubs, attended the same parties, and sent their children to the same colleges; and the poorer whites, who had not been to college, did not own land, and worked for hourly wages. The one thing the two classes had in common was a belief in their superiority to the Negro.

The courtroom, seething with sweat-drenched bodies, was packed. September is one of the hottest months in the Delta, and this year was no exception. The men were in shirt-sleeves, some with ties, but none wearing coats. Four ceiling fans stirred the hot air, offering little relief. Cane chairs had been brought in to accommodate the overflow. Grown men sat in the open windows. Most of the audience was white, and most were friends of the defendants. In the very back of the room stood a tight row of black people. A wooden rail, called the bar, separated the onlookers from the trial's active participants. Inside the bar, there were seats for the presiding judge, the jury, the defendants, their lawyers, the state prosecutors, and two tables for the white press—where Flossie and Betty were to sit. The court stenographer was the only other woman seated inside the bar. A card table for the black reporters was stuck to one side outside the bar, separated.

As Betty took her seat, the judge's gavel, pounding for order, stilled the stifling courtroom. Defendant Roy Bryant's two-year-old toddler, sitting on his father's lap, jumped down, crawled under the bar, and ran back to his mother, sitting in the first row of the visitor's section. Thirty-six-year-old Milam sat next to Bryant, his twenty-four-year-old half-brother. Their mother had two husbands and eleven children; five boys were Milams, and three girls and three boys were Bryants. All were closely bound in what William Bradford Huie described as "a lusty and devoted clan that stuck together." The family operated a chain of cotton field stores, which sold trucks and mechanical cotton pickers. Milam, who had been a platoon leader a decade before in World War II, still had a strong, athletic body. Both men, clean-shaven and wearing starched white shirts unbuttoned at the collars, appeared relaxed. Jury selection took all of the first day. As the jurors were seated, Betty watched the expressions on their faces and whispered to Flossie, "They'll never convict." Even if the jury had been impartial, she realized that a conviction after that trial—which increasingly resembled a scripted theater piece—was almost impossible.

The presiding judge, Curtis Swango, kept a tight reign on a potentially explosive situation and ran the trial informally, "with grace and gentility," according to the *New York Post*'s Murray Kempton. But it was Sheriff Strider, lording over the entire proceedings, who claimed center stage. Clarence Strider was an imposing man, weighing in at two hundred seventy pounds. He was a wealthy landowner, whose property could be identified from miles away by the letters S-T-R-I-D-E-R painted on the roofs of sharecroppers' shacks. Strider believed that it was "those niggers from the North" that were causing all the trouble, and before the trial began, he issued an edict declaring that no Negroes would be admitted into the courtroom. Strider tried to bar Charles Diggs, a black congressman from Detroit, who had accompanied Emmett Till's mother from Chicago. When Betty's friend, the ex-sheriff Harry Dogan, saw what was happening, he walked up to Strider and quietly said, "Clarence, let him in. If you think you are having media problems, just try telling a United States Congressman he can't go into the courthouse, and you'll find out what a real problem is." During the trial, Strider took the witness stand to testify for the defense, and he refused to identify the body as Till's or to state a cause of death. Bill Minor, covering the trial for the *New Orleans Times-Picayune*, later wrote, "The atmosphere of the courtroom was such that it was a foregone conclusion that they [Bryant and Milam] would be acquitted, with Swango doing his best to hold up the standards of justice."

Sensing the virulent mood in the courtroom—and sensing the anger and mistrust of her Sumner friends—Betty became even more determined to show the visiting reporters all Southerners did not hate Negroes. She was surprised that not one friend phoned her during that week to ask about the trial. It seemed everyone thought that if they turned their backs and ignored the whole thing, "it would just go away." During the lunch break that first day, Betty invited some of the reporters to come out to Rainbow, the Pearsons' plantation, that evening for a casual supper and a chance to relax away from the highly charged atmosphere of the trial and the cold reception they were receiving in town. She wanted these Yankees to experience another side of the Delta, the land and people she loved. But her invitation was more than a gesture of southern hospitality. She craved honest, open conversation about what was happening in the trial; no one in town would talk about it.

Five or six of the reporters came that night and every night for the rest of the week, until the trial ended. The reporters arrived at Rainbow in late afternoon, used the phone to call in their stories, ate dinner, and talked, talked, talked. There was plenty of beer, and Johnny Desmond, the reporter for the *Daily News*, always brought a bottle of bourbon. Ed Clark, the photographer from *Life* magazine, came every afternoon, along with Johnny Popham, who became a lifelong friend of the Pearsons. John N. Popham, based in Chattanooga, was the first Southern correspondent for the *New York Times*. He later became managing editor of the *Chattanooga Times* (owned by the *New York Times*), and over the next two decades earned a reputation as "journalism's point man" in the civil rights movement.

Betty remembers that on the second morning of the trial, soon after the final juror was selected, the prosecution surprised onlookers by abruptly asking for a recess. District Attorney Gerald Chatham, assisted by Special Prosecutor Robert B. Smith III, wanted to call two young black men who earlier said they had witnessed the murder. Judge Swango granted the recess, but the witnesses could not be found. The buzz among the press corps was that Sheriff Strider had the two sequestered in the jail in Charleston, Mississippi, twenty miles away. After an hour, the court reconvened and Strider announced with authority, "They are not in my jail."

Mose Wright, Till's great-uncle, with whom the boy had stayed during his Mississippi visit, gave the most dramatic and damaging testimony of the trial when he pointed his finger directly at Milam and Bryant, identifying them as the two who came to his house in the middle of the night with pistol and flashlight to carry Emmett away. His testimony was clear and direct. When questioned by District Attorney Chatham, Wright said he'd gone to bed with his wife about one o'clock. About two o'clock someone came to the front door shouting, "Preacher, preacher." Wright asked who was there and was told, "This is Mr. Bryant. I want to talk to you and that boy." When Wright opened the door, J. W. Milam was standing there with a pistol in his right hand and a flashlight in his left hand. District Attorney Chatham said, "Now stop there a minute, Uncle Mose. I want you to point out Mr. Milam if you see him here." "There he is," Wright said, and pointed at J. W. Milam. "And do you see Mr. Bryant in here?" Wright pointed directly at Roy Bryant. Murray Kempton, covering the trial for the *New York Post* reported, "[Wright] was taking a tremendous risk by pointing that shaky finger at them. Any drunk could have burnt him out." To prevent such retaliation after he testified, Mose Wright was whisked away by car to Memphis, where he caught a plane to Chicago. Neither he nor his wife, Sue, ever returned to Mississippi.

Wright's testimony left no doubt that early in the morning of August 28, 1955, Bryant and Milam, carrying a flashlight and pistol, entered the Wrights' house, went to the room where Emmett slept, woke him, told him to get dressed, then loaded him into a car and drove away. That was the last time Mose Wright saw his nephew alive. Betty still marvels at Mose Wright's mettle: "It is hard to imagine today, how courageous it was in 1955 for an elderly black man to make that kind of accusation. The Emmett Till murder, and especially his mother's courage in showing the world what had happened to her son, was, I believe, the catalyst for the civil rights movement."

On September 23, 1955, after five full days of testimony from a bevy of witnesses, closing arguments from both the prosecution and defense attorneys, and instructions from Judge Swango, the all-white male jury sitting in the Tallahatchie Court House in Sumner, Mississippi, deliberated just over an hour before acquitting both defendants for the kidnapping and murder of Emmett Till, a fourteen-year-old boy from Chicago. After the trial a juror said, "It wouldn't have taken that long if we hadn't stopped to drink a soda." This verdict would shape the course of Betty Bobo Pearson's future. What she witnessed during the trial thrust her into a new and disturbing awareness that would eventually tear her away from her family, make her suspect in her community, and estrange her from the man who had been the hero of her known world: her father, Robert E. Bobo.

Four months later, on January 24, 1956, *Look* magazine published the confessions of J. W. Milam and Roy Bryant, who admitted to kidnapping and murdering Emmett Louis Till. They were paid $4,000 for their participation in the story written by William Bradford Huie. Having been found not guilty, Milam and Bryant were protected by the double jeopardy clause in the Fifth Amendment of the United States Constitution, prohibiting anyone from being prosecuted twice for the same crime.

# The Beginning

*I am the sixth Robert Eager Bobo. My roots are deep in this land.*
   —Robert Eager Bobo IV

*People who came from the dirt, the land gentry, were the backbone of the South. . . .*
   —Tunkie Saunders

## 1834

When Spencer Bobo, the first Bobo to put down stakes in Mississippi's Coahoma County, arrived in 1834, dense forests of giant oak, hickory, loblolly pine, and chestnut trees, with nearly impassible underbrush, covered the vast expanse of the river's delta, the alluvial plain three hundred miles north of the Mississippi River's mouth. Flocks of blue herons and wood storks nested in the swamp among the cypress. The forests were alive with scavenging black bears, fleet-footed white-tailed deer, squirrels in the trees, skunks on the ground, beavers, raccoons, and red fox everywhere. At night, black panthers—*Coahoma* in Choctaw language—roamed the county that bore their name.

The human inhabitants of these same lands, the Native Americans who for centuries lived beside the great Mississippi ("Father of Waters" in their language), were being summarily removed to Indian Territory in Oklahoma. The soil of the original, seaboard colonies was wearing out. The powers in Washington, DC, dedicated to "expanding the opportunities" and providing land and protection for their new nation's citizens, were successful in gaining control of tribal lands. To compensate the native inhabitants, Congress passed the Removal Act of 1830, establishing a process whereby the president could grant land west of the Mississippi River to Indian tribes that agreed to give up their homelands. The Choctaw Nation in 1830, and the Chickasaw Nation in 1832, ceded their lands east of the Mississippi to the federal government.

Bobo and his family were among the thousands upon thousands of settlers from the original southern seaboard colonies who flocked to this new area seeking a fresh start. Fortunes could be made by planting cotton in the rich, virgin soil. During the first half of the nineteenth century, the state of Mississippi symbolized the promise of American life for all those white Americans who settled there. But before cotton could be planted, the land had to be cleared. Black slaves were brought overland or shipped up the river to perform this backbreaking work. These slaves literally pulled whole forests up by the roots, tilled the soil, and planted cotton, the "green gold" that would then be shipped down the river through New Orleans and across the seas to the textile mills of England, or carried by ship up the eastern seaboard to the industrial states in New England. In the next two decades, the promise of the Mississippi Delta came to fruition. In *River of Dark Dreams*, Walter Johnson shows that the leading edge of the global economy in the nineteenth century was the "capital-importing and cotton-exporting" Mississippi valley. The planters of the Mississippi Delta grew very rich; it was wealth built on the devastation of an enslaved race of people and on Native American disenfranchisement.

Upon arriving in Coahoma County, Spencer and his wife, Louise, quickly forgot the hardships of their arduous trek by horse, mule, and wagon to the untamed wilderness. Traveling over six hundred miles of mud and dust from South Carolina to the Mississippi Delta, they slaughtered a passel of turkeys every day for food. Spencer's brother, Fincher—with his wife, Sara, and their three children (the oldest child, Robert Eager, was Betty's future great-grand-father)—followed in 1850, carving out their own piece of prosperity in Coahoma County. Spencer and Fincher Bobo were fulfilling the dream of their grandfather, Sampson Bobo, of La Rochelle, France (where the name was spelled Beau Beau, Bobogh or Beaubais). Sampson was a Protestant Huguenot who fled Catholic persecution in the late 1700s to become a patriot in the American Revolution. Spencer and Fincher remembered how, when they were young boys in South Carolina, their grandfather urged them to chase every opportunity, establish themselves, and prosper in their new country. Sampson Bobo would be proud of the Bobos of Coahoma County.

The 1860 census recorded the population of Coahoma County and Clarksdale to be 6,606 whites and 5,085 slaves. Cotton, rich soil, and slaves created tremendous wealth for the entire region, and the well-established Bobos flourished—until the 1860s. The Civil War, followed by Reconstruction, demolished this prosperity, along with the social graces and grandeur associated with the life of land-owning whites in Coahoma County. Their wealth was gone. Their slaves were free. Destitute landholders grubbed for bare essentials, battling to hold onto any fragment of their former life. Violence erupted. A Bobo neighbor killed an-other neighbor over a disputed piece of property. Dislocated former slaves struggled to build new, free lives. The times were harsh for everyone.

Yet, even during those troubled times, rules of civility,

religious precepts, and respect for law and order—among both blacks and whites in Coahoma County—undergirded efforts to rebuild a civilized community. In 1869, only four years after the defeat of the Confederacy, a town plan was proposed for Clarksdale, seventy-six uniform blocks on eight streets situated around a large town square. The Bobo name appears prominently both among those who planned the township and in the area's subsequent history.

## The Colonel and Anna

**1868**

Five miles south of the proposed town of Clarksdale, Betty's great-grandfather, Colonel Robert Eager Bobo, who served in the Confederate army, planted his crops and worked to rebuild his life. The year before the plan for the township was adopted, he married Anna Prince of Memphis. On November 24, 1868, the *Memphis Daily Appeal* announced, "A truly worldly and deserving gentleman, never wooed and won a fairer, sweeter prize. . . . A large circle of friends, of which she was a particular star, will miss her gentle presence, but all join in wishing the young couple long life and much happiness." Having known only the social life of the city, Anna was excited by the promise of romance associated with becoming mistress of a Mississippi plantation married to a handsome colonel. But post-bellum life in the Delta, where she was isolated as a farmer's wife and young mother, was very different for this former belle from the city.

In the years to come, after their two sons Robert (named for his father) and Fincher (named for his grandfather) were born, and Anna was no longer the center of her husband's attentions, the allure of her new life wore thin. The colonel worked long hours and traveled far from home for days, often weeks, at a time. He was not only a savvy farmer, he possessed a sharp eye for financial opportunity, and he earned a reputation as a renowned hunter of wild game. By the 1870s, word was out that the railroads were coming to the Delta, a welcome and greatly anticipated boon for the area. Planters would no longer be dependent on the erratic river to get their cotton to market. Realizing that railroad companies needed solid land on which to lay their tracks, Colonel Bobo wasted no time before setting out in his canoe to find the highest and driest ridges in the region. He staked out over 600 acres of heavily forested land, which he purchased in 1880 for $2 per acre. A savvy entrepreneur, the colonel cultivated and frequently entertained the men responsible for bringing the railroad to the Delta. He persuaded Mr. Norton, the advance man from New Orleans—who regularly traveled through Coahoma County to negotiate the right of way for the Illinois Central—to stay in Bobo whenever he was in the area. Anna enjoyed Mr. Norton's visits. His news of city life in New Orleans, Memphis, and Chicago brought a breath of excitement to the confined routine of her country life.

When the railroad arrived in 1884, not only did the colonel's newly acquired land serve as suitable track bed for the company rails, he gave the railroad right of way through his land, and negotiated a contract to furnish the cypress crossties for building the lines. The deal helped him finance the clearing of more land for cultivation, as well as build a whistle-stop at Bobo. Nearly every plantation in the Delta built a flag-stop where one train a day would stop to take on passengers. Over sixty post offices were established at those flag-stops. Many of these stops, some with an adjoining store, were built with Bobo lumber. The Bobos' fortunes blossomed.

For eight months a year, March through October, Colonel Bobo managed his plantation and finances. But as soon as the crop—primarily cotton—was picked and sold or stored, he turned to his major passion, his hunting retreats in the wild woods, the uncultivated areas of the Delta. At the time of his death, the colonel's obituary stated that he had shot over 304 bears during his life, and that at one time he was reputed to be "the mightiest bear hunter in America." Teddy Roosevelt, planning a trip south, contacted the colonel to arrange a hunt with him, but Colonel Bobo refused. On the dates the president would be in the area, the colonel had plans to go hunting with someone else; he would not cancel on a prior commitment. Throughout the year he rhapsodized—to anyone who would listen—about his annual retreats to his hunting camp, where he stayed for weeks at a time with his servants, his bear dogs, and several wagons loaded with food and drink for the all-male party with which he would camp, hunt, and bond. The colonel was particularly pleased when his two sons were old enough to be initiated into this essential aspect of Southern manhood.

Not everyone in the family enjoyed those hunting retreats. During long, dreary, wet winter months when roads to her house in Bobo were usually impassible, Anna was stuck in the remote farmhouse with no adult companionship other than the servants. Telling the story of her great-grandparents, Betty found it easy to imagine the hardship, abandonment, and boredom her great-grandmother must have felt. In the early 1880s, while Colonel Bobo was off on one of his hunting retreats, Mr. Norton, the railroad agent from New Orleans, paid a visit to Bobo. When the colonel and his two teen-aged sons, Fincher and Robert Eager, came home from their hunt, Anna was gone. The colonel's wife, the mother of his sons, had run off to South America with Mr. Norton. The Bobos heard nothing from Anna for the next twenty years.

## Fincher and Bessie

**1897**

Fincher Bobo, Betty's future grandfather, then in his early thirties, was on the northbound train from New Orleans when it stopped in Amory, Mississippi. A beautiful young woman climbed aboard and told the conductor she was going to Clarksdale. Fincher incapable of taking his eyes off this beauty, wondered whom might she be visiting. He longed to meet this young woman at least ten years his junior, but he hesitated. Fortune had not been kind to Fincher when it came to women. The most important women in his life, the two he had truly loved, brought him great sorrow. When he was fourteen his mother ran off to South America with a railroad man from New Orleans. Then, he was in his mid-twenties when his young wife died, leaving him alone with their infant daughter, Hallie, named for her mother. Fincher adored his little Hallie, but realized it would not be good for a young girl to grow-up in a big house out in the country with only two men as family, himself and Colonel Bobo, now an embittered old man. He sent his daughter Hallie to live with her Garrett grandparents in Arkansas, but he maintained regular contact with her.

In spite of his reservations, Fincher managed to learn the name of this beautiful young lady visiting in Clarksdale and wrangled an introduction. She was Elizabeth Brock, called Bessie. Betty remembers her granddaddy saying, "It was love at first sight," but regrets that she does not remember hearing any stories about Fincher and Bessie's romance and courtship. Their marriage records are lost.

Fincher and Bessie's son Robert Eager (Bob) Bobo III (Betty's future father), was born on April 1, 1901. The colonel, for whom the baby was named, died the next year, and the Bobo plantation passed on to his sons Fincher Gist Bobo and Robert Eager Bobo. Young Hallie frequently visited her father and Bessie and her new cousin Bob, but she continued to live with her Garrett grandparents until she married and set up housekeeping in Arkansas.

In 1896, the population of Clarksdale was fifteen hundred Negroes and five hundred whites. Cotton still defined the culture and economy of the Delta. White folks with land were living the good life, politicians kept the poor whites acquiescent by preaching a cult of white supremacy, and in many parts there seemed to be an easy give-and-take between the races. "The blues" created by black folk was being recognized as a distinctive American art form, and Clarksdale became known as a mecca for music. In 1903, the local newspaper pronounced Clarksdale "the most healthful town on the face of the earth." When W. C. Handy, who lived in Clarksdale from 1903 to 1906, came to town with his Black Knights of Pythias Band, he couldn't believe there was a Negro cashier employed by the "white" Planters Bank.

But this easy give-and-take masked a darker reality. In the early part of the twentieth century, foreign (primarily European) investors began buying up land in order to create huge plantations. Negro farmers, who had acquired small farms after the Civil War, could not compete and sold their lands and became sharecropper/tenants to white, sometimes foreign, plantation owners. By 1901, tenants farmed most of the land in the Delta, and 95 percent of those tenants were Negro. As the white landowning class prospered around cotton, Negroes, disenfranchised and powerless, grew more desperate. Yet, for some years to come the two cultures, although segregated, lived side by side. Black labor supported the whites' good life, while Negroes were sustained through hard times by the strength of their church, their close bonds with one another, and the power of their music.

Around 1905, Fincher received an unexpected phone call and heard his mother's voice for the first time in over two decades. Anna was in New Orleans. Mr. Norton was dead. Fincher's mother, the colonel's long absent wife, now widowed, had cancer and wanted to come home to Bobo to die. Fincher, resentful and still angry over his mother's desertion and his abandonment, steeled himself to say no. But Bessie, his young wife, pleaded, "This is your mother. Of course we will take care of her." Betty's great-grandmother, Anna, came home.

The tremendous empathy and family loyalty Bessie showed for a mother-in-law she had never met deeply influenced Betty. She admired the strength of character Bessie displayed in refusing to accede to her husband's demands. Bessie would, in the years to come, ingrain in her granddaughter, Betty, the same type of moral rectitude, one that went against the established mores of the time. Bessie took her stand for someone who was desperate, powerless, and could not win the battle on her own. Betty believed her grandmother's demonstration of determination and compassion for the helpless was the genesis of her own later convictions and actions that alienated her from her family and friends. She also admired her great-grandmother's spunk, which helped Anna extract herself from an untenable situation and run off to South America.

Betty treasures a trunk, filled with family memorabilia—letters, photographs, and newspaper clippings—now sitting in her living room in California. It is the trunk that her great-grandmother Anna took with her when she escaped to South America, and then brought back with her. Betty finds deep satisfaction in the knowledge that within her lineage is a woman who took action—drastic action—in order to seek a better life when she was treated as a supernumerary. Betty feels these two women, her grandmother Bessie and great-grandmother Anna, provided her with models of courageous strength and a legacy she would emulate in her own life.

Knowing the history of prejudice, violence, pain, mistrust and hypocrisy Negroes experienced in the South and elsewhere, it is sometimes difficult to believe that genuine affection between blacks and whites was possible, or that race, the color of one's skin, was not the sole determinant of how people felt about one another. Shortly after Bessie and Fincher married and she moved to the big farm house at Bobo, Bessie saw a young black girl wandering along the railroad tracks, looking lost. Bessie stepped outside to talk with the girl, learned her name was Ilou, and invited her inside. Ilou lived with and worked for the Bobos for the next thirty years.

Ilou was there with Bessie when Bob, Betty's father, was born in 1901. Ilou loved and claimed baby Bob as her own, helping to rear him and declaring he was "my baby." The two developed a deep connection—some might say a supernatural connection. After Bob lied about his age and, at sixteen, joined the Navy during World War I, he was sent overseas. Ilou maintained she sensed their connection the entire time he was gone, despite the thousands of miles of separation.

No one was happier than Ilou when, at war's end in 1918, Bob came home to Bobo. He had not finished high school. However, every returning veteran who had not yet graduated before he enlisted automatically received a high school diploma upon discharge, making it possible to go to college. After returning to Clarksdale, Bob attended Ole Miss for a couple of years until he and Lenora Olive Corley married in 1920. Lenora, a small, stylish beauty three years older than Bob, also had deep roots in the Delta. The Corley lands, where Lenora grew up, were near Farrell, a few miles west of Clarksdale and nearer the Mississippi River. Bob and Lenora had known each other since high school, and their friends were not surprised when the handsome couple announced their engagement.

Although materially secure, Lenora's young life had not been easy. One of six children, she was nine years old when her mother died of scarlet fever. A few months later, her father was holding one of Lenora's younger brothers in his arms while he watched a smoke stack being raised at a cotton gin on his land. The structure collapsed. As the tower began to fall, Mr. Corley threw the child out of harm's way, but he himself was crushed and died. Corley relatives stepped in, wanting to help by dividing the six children among themselves, but Dick, the oldest Corley son, then in his teens, insisted the family stay together. A Mrs. Marshall was hired and moved into the big house in Farrell to care for the family as surrogate mother until all of the children had received some higher education.

Lenora graduated from Mississippi State College for Women in Columbus about the time Bob returned home from the war. Soon after their wedding, Bob and Lenora moved to Forest Hill, Tennessee, where Bob managed a dairy his father had acquired in a land swap. Ilou remained with Bessie and Fincher at Bobo, but her deep connection with "her baby," was still evident when Lenora became pregnant. One morning in mid-May, Ilou announced to Bessie she was quitting her job. Ilou had been with Bessie for over twenty years, and in shock, she asked, "Why in the world, Ilou? Is something wrong?" Ilou responded, "Baby needs me."

Lenora, the expectant mother, never asked for—may not even have wanted—Ilou's assistance. She was totally surprised when Ilou arrived unexpectedly in Forest Hill a day later, found Bob and Lenora's house, and went directly to the back yard. She saw Lenora up on a ladder by a cherry tree, and told her to get down immediately. That night, May 19, 1922, Lenora went into labor. Bob called the doctor (doctors all made house calls in those days), but before he could get there, Ilou delivered a baby girl, Erie Elizabeth (Betty) Bobo. Later, Ilou said, "I just had a feeling I had to get there."

Soon after Betty's birth, the young family and Ilou moved back to Bobo, where Ilou lived in an apartment above the garage, a place Betty remembers well. Her parents drove into Clarksdale for the evening quite often, and on those occasions she and little Bob slept in Ilou's apartment.

Betty was nine when Ilou had a stroke, telling Betty's father she wanted two things when she died: him holding her hand, and a certain Baptist minister to preach at her funeral. Ilou did not recover from the stroke. Three weeks later, Big Bob climbed the steps to her apartment to sit at her bedside and hold her hand until her last breath. Among her belongings, the family found Ilou's legacy: two $2,000 insurance policies naming Robert E. Bobo III as beneficiary, with a note attached that read, "Baby, I know you will have a hard time educating Betty and Bob."

# Memories

Memories are selective. Filtered over many years, they pro-
duce our personal myths—the foundation of our characters—and they are not to be discarded lightly. Myths may
be the only true narrative of human experience, the truest
history that shapes our souls.

Betty remembers growing up in the big house surrounded by a loving family and caring servants, a pony to ride,
huge trees to climb, chickens to feed, and lots of land and
open fields to explore. These were surroundings that nur-
tured her free spirit, bold temperament, and tomboy ten-
dencies. Looking back, she feels in many ways she had an
ideal childhood, one without television or organized sports,
and totally unlike anything her grandchildren experienced
later. The first Christmas tree she remembers had real candles because her family home had no electricity. A few years
later, everyone was excited when they got their first radio,
which they listened to through earphones.

Safe and cared for by the people who worked on the farm
and in her grandmother's garden, Betty never wondered
why she lived in a big white house, while her black playmates

lived in small, unpainted cypress cabins. One of those cabins was a short distance down a dusty path from the big house, and the elderly black woman who lived there entertained Betty and her playmates for hours with stories of her life under slavery. Too young to understand the significance of these stories, Betty thought the old lady was spinning yarns about living in some exotic far away country. In later years she wondered if the black children, who listened with her and her brother, were as confused, or if they knew they were learning a history that would haunt all of them for the rest of their lives.

Until Betty started school and began to find new friends, her little brother, Bob, two years younger, was her closest playmate. She relished her role as big sister, showing him who was boss. A tree house high up in a huge oak behind their house became her private refuge and a wonderful symbol of her superiority over her little brother. When Bob was a small tot, a bit clumsy and not as agile as Betty, he was unable to climb up to that tree house. This arrangement suited Betty. What better way to show her little brother that she was indeed high and mighty? Climbing that huge oak, she sat in her tree house and ignored little Bob's incessant pleas for her to show him how to get up to the tree house. She never did.

Sometimes Betty, Bob, and Big Mama (the name the children called their grandmother Bessie) improvised little conspiracies against Betty's mother, Lenora. Bessie, a hard-headed country girl who grew up in the pines of North Carolina, thought it was perfectly safe—in fact an exciting adventure—for the children to ride on the front fenders of her car to the little country store two long blocks away, if she drove slowly and they held on tight. Their mother disagreed and begged Bessie not to undertake this stunt. On their trips to the store with their grandmother, Betty and Bob would start out riding in the car, but as soon as they were out of sight of the house, Big Mama stopped to let them out, and they climbed on the fenders. It was a daring subterfuge.

The September after her fifth birthday, Betty started kindergarten in Clarksdale, riding a school bus the eight miles into town from Bobo. For the first time in his life, Bob found himself alone at home without his constant playmate. Betty liked school and was eager to pass on her newly acquired knowledge. Every day when she returned home, she set up a classroom for Bob where she taught him everything she had learned that day. The next year, after Betty started first grade, her brother's afternoon lessons became more intense. She really made him study. Bob learned to read and write and add numbers. With a voice filled with pride, Betty recalled that he learned it all and he loved it. When it was time for Bob to start first grade, he was tall for his age, and since he could already read and do sums, they tested his aptitude. He started school in second grade. Betty enjoyed her role in her little brother's education.

After her eighth birthday, Betty spent at least a month every summer on the Gulf Coast with her Aunt Erie, Betty's mother's sister, and Uncle Raymond. The couple had no children and enjoyed spoiling their independent-minded little niece. She wanted to learn to sail, and though she later questioned whether either her aunt or her uncle knew anything about boats, when she was fourteen they bought her a sailboat. It was a broad beam catboat, eighteen feet long with a thirty-foot-high mast and shallow draft. Looking back, Betty thinks it was probably better suited to lake sailing than to the strong winds and seasonal squalls in the Gulf of Mexico. Never one to shy away from a challenge, she learned to sail her boat and loved it. Her aunt dropped her off at the yacht club in the mornings, where there were lots of kids her age, and Betty spent all day, every day on the water. The young sailors, ignoring their instructions to keep in sight of the yacht club, headed out five to ten miles offshore to open water, often dropping sail when a storm hit. Even with lightning striking all around, Betty remembered, they were never afraid.

Back home in Clarksdale, the October 30, 1935, edition of the school newspaper, "The Spotlights," reported the results of the eighth grade Who's Who contest: most popular girl, Betty Bobo; best sport girl, Betty Bobo; smartest girl, Betty Bobo; best all-round girl, Betty Bobo.

Summertime was an ever-unfolding adventure. Camp Tallaha, the regional Boy Scout camp near Clarksdale, opened for girls late in the summer. She was nine years old the first time she went to Tallaha and loved everything about it, especially roaming the woods near the camp. The first summer she was there, Betty, a total tomboy, caught a king snake and put it in her shirt, waiting until everyone sat down to lunch in the mess hall to pull it out. Pandemonium—what a bunch of screaming ten-to-fifteen-year-old girls!

Betty relished her climb to the tree house at Bobo, and she found the rafters in the camp's rec hall equally challenging. Bob Bailey, a longtime friend from Sumner several years younger than Betty, remembered being at Tallaha one summer. He walked into the rec hall, looked up through the rafters and saw "Betty Bobo" printed in big, bold letters on the ceiling. Filled with confidence and spunk, Betty had made her mark. No one else she'd ever known had been thrown from a speeding train and lived to tell about it.

The summer she was thirteen, Betty went to Camp Lake Lure in North Carolina for six weeks. She did not like that camp nearly as much as she liked Tallaha, but one incident that occurred there remains locked in her memory. A group of campers loaded onto a bus for a field trip, then stopped beside a bridge high above a river. Betty and four or five of the other girls walked out on the bridge and started talking about how high they were, wondering what would happen if someone jumped into the river below. Betty said she wouldn't mind doing that. The girls kept talking, egging each other on, until one said, "If you don't mind, I dare you to jump." Betty climbed over the rail and jumped with no idea of the depth of the water. Every counselor on the bus scrambled down the hill as fast as possible to be at the water's edge when Betty surfaced and swam to shore. Fortunately, the river was deep enough, and she didn't hit a rock—but she did incur the wrath of every adult on that trip. Not one of the grim-faced counselors spoke a word to her as she climbed back on the bus and rode back to camp in wet clothes.

Betty said she never understood what happened on the last day of camp, the award day at Camp Lake Lure. There were three major awards: one for love, one for loyalty, and one for leadership. She did not believe her ears when her name was called as the winner of the leadership award. Even though she'd been runner-up for the camp's tennis championship and received a marksmanship medal for rifle shooting, the most notice she'd received that summer was for things the counselors did not want their campers to do. Now, she was awarded a silver bracelet inscribed with the year and the word "Leadership." Proud of her bracelet, Betty was terribly disappointed when it was stolen that fall at Clarksdale High.

Frank Mitchener remembers the summer Betty taught him to swim when she was a lifeguard at the Clarksdale civic center pool. He said she threw him in the deep end and yelled for him to swim to the side. He did. Betty recalled the incident differently. She said Mother Pearl, Frank's mother, brought six-year-old Frank to the pool and asked her to teach him to swim. As soon as his mother released Frank's hand, he ran to the deep end and jumped in. Betty immediately dove in, pulled him out, and took him to the shallow end, where the swimming lessons began. Memories are very selective.

Betty's father was her hero; she could always count on him. She did not know whether it was so, but Betty believed she was his favorite: "I was his and he was mine." If she got in trouble, Big Bob just laughed and took up for her. There was the time when she was in high school and found a list of all the lockers, up and down the halls of Clarksdale High, including each locker number, the name of the person who used the locker, and the locker's combination. After Betty shared her discovery with her good buddy Frank Ralston, the two friends decided it would be great fun to switch all the locks during lunch hour. They did, creating a total fracas when the rest of the students returned after lunch and could not open their lockers. Mr. McGivren, the school principal—knowing Betty's reputation not only as an outstanding student, but also as a prankster—called her into his office to ask if she had anything to do with the incident. Betty confessed; she could not tell a lie. And what did her daddy do when he heard about the locker lock switch? He laughed.

Betty and Frank Ralston executed another prank, and this time they did not get caught. Every Friday morning, chapel was held in the high school's auditorium, a large room with a high shelf-like ledge on three walls. Busts of famous people, such as George Washington, Socrates, and Shakespeare, were placed on the ledge. One Friday morning, Frank and Betty collected as many alarm clocks as they could find and set the alarms to go off at five-minute intervals. Before chapel that day, they snuck into the auditorium and placed a clock behind each bust. After the student body assembled, the opening prayer was given and the pledge of allegiance recited. The speaker for the day was introduced. As he walked to the podium, the first alarm went off. He paused, waited for the ringing to stop, and began to speak. Five minutes later, another alarm sounded—then another and another, throughout the hour. The students found it uproarious good fun. The speaker must have been a good sport. Those responsible never came under suspicion—or at least they were never punished.

The memory that defined Betty's future happened one summer day when she was seven or eight. The house at Bobo had a wide screen porch across the front, where her mother and her grandmother Bessie, busy with their needlework, sat and chatted. Betty and Bob sprawled at the opposite end of the porch, building a fort with upturned porch chairs. Ilou's voice called through an open window: "Miz Lenora, some un's at the back door, and my hands is deep in dough." Betty's mother, looking up from her stitchery, asked Betty to run see who it was. Betty ran, returned, and reported, "Mama, there's a lady who wants to see you." When Lenora came back to the porch, she slowly lowered her self into her rocker, looked directly at Betty and said in a low, distinct voice, "Betty that was no lady, that was a Negro woman—only white people are called lady." The next morning, when Betty and her grandmother were alone outside in the garden, Big Mama said, "Little Sis, I have something I need to tell you. I hate to contradict your mother, but what she told you yesterday afternoon is not true. A person is a lady if she acts like a lady. Being black or white has nothing to do with it."

Betty said that day a seed was planted that grew into her later quarrel with segregation and the idea of racial superiority. Her grandmother Bessie also told her stories about white men who had Negro mistresses, and wives who knew their white children had Negro half-brothers and -sisters. Betty's grandmother never said whether these relationships were right or wrong. There was nothing in her stories about the horrors of miscegenation that colored the whispered conversations that Betty overheard. Betty was never sure what her grandmother believed, but Bessie was always loving and non-judgmental. Her message was that all people are equal. Elizabeth (Bessie) Brock Bobo, her paternal grandmother, whom Betty called Big Mama, was one of two people most influential in her life.

The other truly influential person in her life was her father. Here is Betty's own assessment of him, taken from the book *Pieces from the Past*, edited by Joan Sadoff:

> [My father was] a strong man, very much the extrovert, a
> leader who genuinely liked people. He taught me to ride
> and to hunt and he encouraged independence of spirit.
> He was as honest a man as I've ever known; he taught my
> brother and me to be responsible for our own behavior and
> to always do what we knew was right, no matter what our
> peers thought—a lesson that back-fired in the 1960s when
> what I thought was right differed so much from his own
> values. I adored him. The most painful thing for me during
> the civil rights days was that in standing against segrega-
> tion, I was standing against my father. Following his death,
> it was a great comfort when Aaron Henry [the head of
> the local NAACP] called and said, "Betty, your father was
> a good man. His office was one of the few in Clarksdale
> I could enter knowing I would be treated with respect. I
> know that you disagree with him about race, but just re-
> member that he was the product of his upbringing."

I found that willingness to understand and forgive in

many of the black leaders of the movement. My father's "upbringing" meant that he was good to the black people who worked for him, but it was always a paternalistic relationship. He took care of them in the way he took care of his children. Underneath was the firmly held belief that black people were innately inferior to whites.

All of the schools I attended, including college, were of course segregated. As I grew older I no longer had black friends my age, although we always had a black cook, a black gardener, and a black man who drove my grandmother. An interesting tidbit about the segregated schools at that time is the different meaning given to "colored" in different Delta towns. In Clarksdale the Chinese children were sent to the black schools, while in Sumner they went to the white schools. By the time I went off to college in the fall of 1940, I was sure in my belief that a segregated society was wrong and that people were just people, regardless of skin color.

In the boom years of 1918 and 1919, a Delta planter had so much money he didn't know what to do with it, but a decade later the Great Depression of the 1930s devastated many of those same farmers. During those economically difficult times, Betty's father decided the Bobo land could not support his family. He took a job with the Delta Grocery and Cotton Company and moved his family to Clarksdale, where they lived for a couple of years in a rented house. By the time Betty graduated from high school and was deciding where to go to college, the family had moved back to Bobo. Money was still tight. Her father said she would have to attend a state-supported college. That was all he could afford. Betty signed up for the state school in Starkville, while applying at the same time for a scholarship to Millsaps, a small, selective liberal arts college in Jackson, Mississippi. With her outstanding academic and leadership record, Betty received a four-year, full-tuition scholarship to Millsaps.

In her freshman year at Millsaps, Betty made many new friends—one in particular. Florence "Flossie" Mars, from Philadelphia, Mississippi, a spirited, headstrong young woman with a slight limp, became her best friend. Flossie and Betty enjoyed the same things, played tennis almost every morning before class, and spent hours in the record shop on State Street listening to the big band music of Artie Shaw, Louie Armstrong, Tommy Dorsey, Glenn Miller, and Count Basie.

These two young women, Flossie from the hill country of Mississippi and Betty from the Delta, shared the same values in almost everything—and they both would become outspoken voices in the civil rights struggle. However, there was one area in which they did not agree: money management. Flossie felt Betty's people's attitude towards their money was downright immoral. Delta people farmed, lived on credit, and paid their bills in the fall when their crops were harvested and sold. This practice horrified Florence. People from the hill country would never buy on credit. An honorable person would never go into debt. If you couldn't afford it, you couldn't buy it. Betty felt that her and her best friend's opposing attitudes about finance taught her an important lesson: two fundamentally good people can hold totally different views on an important issue. She was thankful to have learned this lesson when, later on, she and her father held very different views about civil rights.

At the beginning of her sophomore year, Betty suffered acute appendicitis and required an emergency operation. The surgeon not only took out her appendix, but also discovered and removed a diseased ovary. Her extensive operation obliged Betty to endure several months of convalescence. She missed the entire first semester of her second year. Millsaps did not offer first semester courses during the spring, so she would have to wait until the following September to re-start her sophomore year. This schedule was not a good option for this bright, energetic, take-charge, find-the-action, young woman. Too much was happening. Pearl Harbor had been bombed in December; her country was at war. Fellows she knew from high school had already joined the service.

In fact, a friend she'd dated in high school and who was attending Georgia Tech, enlisted in the Army immediately after the United States declared war. When home for a few weeks at Christmas before reporting for duty, he called Betty for a date and proposed marriage almost as soon as he picked her up. He was convinced that he was going to be killed in battle, and his one desire was to leave an heir to carry on his name. He pleaded for Betty to marry him before he was sent overseas. Hardly ready to marry, Betty did not accept his proposal. (He survived the war, came home to the Delta, married, and raised three daughters.)

If she could not return to Millsaps until the following September, she knew she could not wait nine months to re-start her second year of college. Betty Bobo had to get on with her life. She gave up her scholarship from Millsaps and transferred to the University of Mississippi to restart her sophomore year in the spring of 1942. Flossie, not wanting to lose her best friend, transferred to Ole Miss at the same time. She and Betty roomed together for a month, until Betty moved into a room of her own. Betty recalled, "Flossie was a great person, a wonderful friend—but horribly messy."

With the United States involved in World War II, the university offered a full schedule of courses year round. Betty decided to accelerate her academic timetable, taking eighteen to twenty-one hours every semester, working through the summers to graduate in two and a half years. On a torridly hot day in the middle of her first summer semester at Ole Miss, Betty went down to the laundry in the dormitory basement to pick up some clothes. Stepping into the subterranean, oven-like space, she wondered aloud how anyone could stand such heat. Without raising her head the Negro worker behind the counter mumbled, "If you think this is hot, you should go to the back of the laundry where there's no fans. Like being boiled alive. Not making enough money to suffer so." Betty remembers not giving much thought to her response. More to make conversation than deliberately provoke, she suggested the laundry workers go on strike. In such heat, and with the campus full of students, the university could not afford to let the laundry shut down.

Several days later, four black laundry workers found Betty in her dorm room. They told her they had decided to strike and wanted her to go with them to talk to the chancellor and the manager of the laundry. Betty was not eager to comply with their request, but since her suggestion had planted the seed, she felt she had no choice. Seeking moral support, she talked Florence into going with her and the workers to see the chancellor. Their efforts were successful. The laundry workers received a small pay raise, better hours, and the addition of large fans in the back of the laundry. Betty's father received a telephone call from Chancellor Butts, who had been one of his friends in college. Chancellor Butts told Bob Bobo if his daughter did any more labor agitating on campus she would be expelled. The same night, Betty received a call from her very angry parent. He was not laughing.

Shaken and confused, yet pleased for the laundry workers, Betty promised to keep a low profile during the rest of her time at Ole Miss. She kept her promise. She went to class and did well in English, philosophy, psychology, and math. But she was a terrible student if she did not like a course, and her performance suffered in world history and languages. She continued to wonder where and how she fit in. Except for her friendship with Florence, Betty was a loner. Her interests revolved around playing tennis, swimming, and just being by herself. Although there were few bikes on the Ole Miss campus at that time, she and Florence had theirs with them and decided to ride the 330 miles to Gulfport one weekend. Early on a Friday morning they peddled fifty miles south, hauling themselves through the hills on a gravel road to Grenada. After spending that night in a motel, they caught the bus to Jackson the next day and spent the afternoon in their favorite record shop on State Street. They had a grand time, but then decided "So much for Gulfport." After spending Saturday night in Jackson, they tied their bikes to the back of a Greyhound bus the next morning and returned to Oxford.

On a campus famous for its vibrant social life, Betty never felt she belonged. She went to college dances when asked to be someone's date, but she had little interest in what seemed to be the major concerns of most of the coeds: how they looked, who was dating whom, and what to wear to the weekend party. Transferring to Ole Miss in the middle of the year, Betty never synced, never belonged with an in-coming class, never connected to a larger group. She was not a typical college coed. For the first time in her life, Betty Bobo felt like a misfit.

A picture of a severe, non-smiling Betty appears only twice in the 1943 Ole Miss yearbook, which shows her once as a graduating senior, and once as a member of the Chi Omega sorority. The picture on the sorority page was placed before she resigned in disgust when two childhood friends from Clarksdale were blackballed. What a contrast to the 1940 Clarksdale High School yearbook, where Betty Bobo's picture was on almost every page. She was given superstar billing as Miss Clarksdale High, as president (or at least a member) of numerous service and athletic organizations, as well as the hall of fame. She was co-editor of the school newspaper, a key member of the annual staff, and a top-notch student. Betty remembered high school as an immensely happy time. In those days Clarksdale High School was also called Bobo Senior High, since it had been built in 1930 on land the Bobo family gave the township. In fact, a small, fenced-off Bobo family cemetery occupied one corner of the schoolyard.

In high school, Betty was at the center of her wonderful world. She knew everyone. She loved her teachers, loved her coaches, loved her life. Lee McCarty, Betty's friend since high school, spoke of a big holiday party to which kids from all the little towns in the Delta were invited. Betty, wearing a "gorgeous, red velvet dress," was so popular that Lee hardly had one dance with her. The other fellows kept cutting in. But at Ole Miss, Betty felt like an "odd ball," felt she never really fit in.

In a philosophy class during her senior year at the university, students were required to write an essay on a topic of their choosing. Betty turned in a paper entitled "Why Schools Should Be Integrated." Her professor was impressed. Professor Kantz asked her if he could enter her essay in the Rosenthal competition, which awarded the winner with a scholarship to attend graduate school at Columbia University. Betty agreed and thought little more about it. A few months before she graduated, Professor Kantz called her into his office and announced she had won a full scholarship to do graduate work at Columbia. Betty was ecstatic. Graduate school in New York! Any program she wanted to take! She could hardly wait to tell her parents the good news.

"Absolutely not," her father declared. "No daughter of mine is going to live in New York City. There is no way I'll allow my daughter to live in Yankee Land. Absolutely not. No more discussion." Betty had never been more than a few hundred miles from home. Except for a week at a camp in Cincinnati years before, she had never even left the South. Her family consisted of seven generations of Mississippians. Everyone knew who she was. It was simply out of the question. They fought, they argued. Betty cried, Betty begged, Betty slammed doors. Nothing worked. Seventy years later, Betty muses, "Back then, folks didn't live in the same world we live in today. Southern men were very paternalistic. They didn't know what separation meant. My daddy would have been perfectly happy if my brother Bob built a house on one side of our family home, and I built one on the other side. He never understood that at some point children had to be turned loose."

She was furious—and incredibly disappointed—but family loyalty ran deep. Betty turned the scholarship down. The relationship with her father was too important. She could not directly defy his will. However, she was determined to find a way to show him that she was a grown woman, an adult, a college graduate. He could not manage her life forever. Their nation was at war. Over the two previous years, every male her age had enlisted or been called into the military. The Ole Miss campus was teeming with ROTC students, both men and women, wearing uniforms. Betty hit upon a solution to her dilemma. If she were not going to graduate school, she would join the service. "That'll fix him."

In the fall of 1943, shortly after graduating from Ole Miss,

Betty borrowed her mother's car, drove to Memphis, and headed directly to the Sterick Building, which housed two separate recruiting offices—one for the Navy and one for the Marine Corps. Interviewing with both of the services, Betty learned that both offered a commission to college graduates who successfully completed boot camp and officer training school. Betty made a snap decision. The Marine Corps appeal to the young women of the nation to "Be a Marine, Free a Marine to fight" hooked her. Erie Elizabeth Bobo from Clarksdale, Mississippi, volunteered that day for the newly established Marine Corps Women's Reserve. All she had to do was survive boot camp.

Driving home to Clarksdale, where her parents were living, Betty gloated. This would "fix" her father, show him who was in charge of her life. She could hardly wait to tell him and headed directly to the center of town, parked the car, hopped out, and rushed into his office. She shouted, "I've joined the Marines." To her amazement, her father was delighted. Filled with patriotic pride, he thought it the finest thing a daughter of Robert E. Bobo III could have done. With Betty's mother, Lenora, it was a different story. "Southern ladies just don't join the Marine Corps. What am I going to tell my friends?" But Lenora must have changed her mind. A year later, an article in the *Clarksdale Press Register* stated that Mrs. Robert E. Bobo III was chair of the American Legion Committee of Joint Recruitment, organized to encourage and recruit girls to join the military.

Betty freely admits she felt being a Marine gave her a certain cachet, an elite quality. She also mentioned another attribute: in addition to being the proud, the Marines were the *few*. The Corps was the smallest branch of the military services. Growing up, Betty had thrived in a small town, a small high school, and a small college where everyone knew one another. At a larger university, she felt like an "odd ball." At Ole Miss she did not join a single organization. She was a member of Chi Omega for a time only because she had pledged and became active in the sorority at Millsaps. At Ole Miss, she dropped her membership when she found the group not to her liking. For the last two and a half years, Betty had gone her own way, withdrawn into a personally constructed, self-insulated cocoon. Now, with tremendous excitement, she was ready to break out into an entirely new and different existence. She had joined the United States Marines.

# The Marines

*Joining the Marines was one of the best things I ever did in my life.*
—Betty Bobo Pearson

In 1943, in the midst of World War II, Americans and their allies around the world focused on one goal—winning the war—which meant defeating Nazi Germany and imperial Japan, preserving freedom, the independence of their nations, and their respective ways of life. The United States was totally mobilized. All American men between the ages of eighteen and forty-five were subject to the military draft. Many young men and women—some over forty-five—volunteered to serve. There was a unity of purpose throughout the land.

Every family had someone or knew someone serving in combat overseas. Small silk banners bearing a blue star, signifying that a member of the household served in the military, hung in the windows of millions of homes across the nation. If the star was gold, a family member had been killed in action. Persuasive posters, urging Americans to unite, join in the fight, were ubiquitous in shop windows and on street corners in every American city and small town. One poster seen everywhere pictured a severe-looking Uncle Sam wearing a top hat banded with a single star and pointing his finger, saying, "I want YOU for [the] US Army." Another poster, equally popular, featured a determined young woman, her hair in a red kerchief and sleeves rolled up in order to show her large biceps, saying, "We can do it!"

Many women on the home front became factory workers, mounting the machines that produced armaments, airplanes, and tanks to help win the war. Others volunteered in various capacities in the Red Cross. USO (United Service Organizations) volunteers entertained the military away from home, or met troop trains as they rolled through small towns in the middle of the night, offering coffee and doughnuts to service personnel passing through. Students from kindergarten through high school brought their dimes to school once a week to buy war saving stamps. Grandparents gave their grandchildren war bonds for Christmas. Gasoline, rubber, shoes, and sugar were rationed. Families planted victory gardens and planned their days around morning and evening broadcasts that included bulletins from the battlefront. The radio brought the reality of war home.

Although womenfolk of her Delta society found the idea of joining the military unseemly, Betty responded to something larger. This was her war, and she wanted to contribute, be a part of the cause so much bigger than herself. She needed to help destroy evil. Betty Bobo acted completely on her own when she joined the Marines. She wanted to demonstrate to her father that she was an adult and would make her own decisions about her life, but she also felt compelled to do all she could do for a noble cause. She wanted to commit her efforts to the greater purpose in which she passionately believed: her nation's freedom. Cultural and family traditions did not stop Betty Bobo from volunteering for the Marines. She feels the acting on her own initiative, as well as what she learned about herself and others while in the Marines, gave her the courage to stand up to her parents and most of white Mississippi society in support of another great cause, the fight to end racial segregation in her beloved homeland.

In the Marines nobody knew her family. "In the Delta, not only did everyone know you, they knew your parents, your grandparents, your aunt, your uncle who drank too much, they know everything about you. In the Marines they know nothing about you. What you do depends on you. It's a great place to grow up." Betty would be absolutely on her own for the first time in her life, away from Mississippi and her family, but informed with newfound independence.

On a blustery winter day in late February of 1944, Betty and her parents drove the eighty miles north from Clarksdale to the Illinois Central Railroad station in Memphis, a long block east of the tall bluff overlooking the Mississippi River. The cavernous depot bustled with activity. As the Bobo threesome made their way across the marble floor, Lenora's high heels, which made her the same height as her daughter but still a head shorter than her husband, clicked sharply with each step. Reaching the crowded platform, Betty kissed her parents good-bye, bounded onto the train, and found a seat among a group of other young women. They were volunteers from points west—Arkansas, Oklahoma, Texas, New Mexico, Arizona, and California. Recruits from the northwest, the central heartland, and the northeast were on other trains, but they were all headed for Camp Lejeune in North Carolina.

When the Women Reserve Corps was organized the year before, General Holcombe, the Corps commandant, ruled out "cute titles." Female Army recruits were WACS, and the Navy's were WAVES. Female Marine recruits were to be called Marines. Holcombe declared, "They will get their basic training in a Marine atmosphere at a Marine post. They inherit the traditions of Marines. They are Marines."

All new Marine recruits were ordered to report to Camp Lejeune at New River, North Carolina. According to the *Women in Military Service for America Memorial Foundation*, the switch from civilians to Marines began before their arrival. From across the nation, about five hundred recruits per troop train first traveled to Wilmington, North Carolina. "At the depot, they were lined up, issued paper armbands identifying them as boots (trainees), and ordered to pick up luggage—anybody's luggage—and marched aboard another train. At the other end, shouting NCOs [noncommissioned officers] herded them to austere barracks with large, open squad-bays, group shower rooms, male urinals, and toilet stalls without doors. No time was allowed for adjustment. A few wondered what they had done and why they had done it."

But Betty never entertained any doubts; she was cut out to be a leatherneck. From the moment she signed up in the recruiting office, she was totally dedicated to being the best possible Marine. Her heart swelled with patriotism, as did her father's. He would not allow her to leave the South to study in New York, but he had enthusiastically endorsed her volunteering to serve her country in time of war. This was an honorable Bobo tradition. During World War I, he had joined the Navy when he was sixteen.

We do not have to rely on Betty's memory in describing her enthusiasm for the Marines when she was twenty-two years old. Her feelings are captured in her first letter home to her parents from Camp Lejeune. Today Betty keeps this letter, along with other cherished memorabilia, in the trunk, which now sits in the living room of her apartment in the University Retirement Village in Davis, California. It is the trunk her great-grandmother Anna brought back to Bobo from South America over a hundred years ago.

March 1, 1944

Dearest Mother and Dad,

Our first week of boot camp was over today. It has passed by awfully quickly, yet it seems like I've been here all may life. I got my first mail today—five letters. I had begun to believe they were never going to start coming. Mail is really a big help

Yesterday we went to sickbay for our physicals. I had just come sick and so was not feeling so hot anyway (although the esercys [sic] or something has straightened me out. I didn't have cramps). They gave us a typhoid shot, a tetanus shot and a vaccination, and I really had a reaction. About seven o'clock I went to bed with chills and fever. But although the N.C.O.s are strict, they are really swell to us. Corporal Kelly came up with extra blankets and hot water bottles and gave me dope to run my temperature down. She's wonderful—I needed a little attention about then. And today I feel fine.

This is really the most interesting experience I've ever had in my life. There are girls here from ever part of the county, and of course all kinds. Two I like especially— Frances Bulla is from Oklahoma. She's in VI-A, has a Masters degree. Margie Drake is from St. Louis and is really a swell kid. She's "Admiral" Drake and I'm "Colonel" Bobo.

I'm pretty proud of myself for having gone a week with no demerits. They give them for everything—quarters not absolutely spotless, late in formation, talking in ranks, not "sounding off" to an N.C.O. or officer. With each demerit goes an hour's EPO—extra police duty. That could be guard duty (the entire area is patrolled all night by shifts) or some cleaning detail. Of course you get cleaning details whether you get a demerit or not, but the demerits go down on your record. For example, I was the first one through with the medical, so they gave me a broom, brush, and mop and I had to clean the heads at the sickbay. Then take all the wastebaskets about six blocks down the street and empty them!

We've about got our schedules set up—at 5:45 calisthenics, dress, and clean the barracks by 6:50, breakfast at 7. Classes begin at 8 and last all morning. Classes, phys ed., and drill after lunch. From 4:30 till 5:30 we can wash clothes, etc. then chow. Free time till 7:30, then quiet hours till 9, have to stay in the squad room and be quiet. In bed by 9:50. We have Friday afternoons, Sat. nights and Sundays off, but that doesn't mean anything. There's always either EPD, a cleaning detail, a GI party or extra drill. If you get any time off, you can go to the PX in squads of 10, march over & back, and only 30 min. from the time you check out till you're back in . . . not much time and we've had to start studying now.

I'm a drilling dude. Corp. Kelly said the best in the platoon. We'd better win the banner for excellent close order drill—I've bet next month's pay on it.

We got our uniforms fitted Monday morning. We will get them probably a week from Friday. We are wearing our uniform caps now and have to salute officers. I haven't become used to that yet.

I took out $10,000 insurance and made Toad [Betty's nickname for her mother] my beneficiary. It costs $6.60 per month. Please try to explain to all the people I should write how very busy I am. I have written a letter a day, and will make the rounds, but it will take time.

Mother, if you're in Memphis, see if any of the stores carry official MCWR bags. Be sure it's our official bag, and if it is, buy me one and keep it for me. They don't issue them any more, but you have to have one, & they're scarce.

Unlike the Army & Navy, no publicity about the Marine Corps may be published without the Public Relations Dept.'s sanction. So if one of our society page reporters asks about me, you can tell them I'm at boot camp here, but nothing I tell you about my activities can be printed. Don't forget that because they raise hell if anyone disobeys that order. Better quit and hit the sack. I'm always asleep on my feet by 9:30. Write often—I love hearing from you. And don't worry about me. I've never enjoyed anything any more in my life.

Lots of love,

Betty

To bring the women's training, as much as possible, in line with that of male Marines, the Corps adopted the system used in the men's OCS (officer candidate school) program at Quantico, Virginia, so women officer candidates at New River were appointed to the rank of private first class. All candidates (both women and men) wore PFC (private first class) chevrons and OC (officer candidate) pins on their lapels and caps. Betty, the "drilling dude" who wore her pins with intense pride, had landed in a different world. While her primary focus, her personal responsibility, was to prove that she was an exemplary Marine, she was meeting contemporaries from completely different social, cultural, and economic backgrounds. Never before had she known anyone whose father worked in a factory, or a motor plant, or a steel mill. The brother of her bunkmate from Cleveland was a union organizer. She was learning interesting stuff that ignited her natural, inborn conviviality.

Erie Elizabeth Bobo not only survived boot camp and officer training, she thrived and received her commission as a second lieutenant in May 1944. Now Betty, a bright, high-spirited scion of a notable Delta family, was a competent officer in the United States Marines. Newly commissioned officers had no say in where they would go or what they would do. This uncertainty was fine with Betty; she belonged in and trusted the Corps. Placed in Marine aviation, she was sent to the Marine airfield in Cherry Point, North Carolina, to await permanent assignment. Every new experience in a vastly different environment was an adventure for this newly minted lieutenant, but one thing in particular stood out. Betty rarely, if ever, saw a Negro. The Marines had begun accepting Negroes at the same time they opened the Corps to women (the year before, in 1943), but Negroes who joined the Marines were placed in all-black units, separated from the other trainees.

While at Cherry Point, Betty ran into Harris Barnes, a friend from Clarksdale. He told her of an incident that reminded her of her hometown and the world she'd left behind. Barnes, a white captain in charge of an all-Negro unit, was checking the mess hall line when he saw one Marine who looked like he'd slept in his uniform. Barnes signaled him out. The recruit, delighted to have an opportunity to speak to his commanding officer, stepped forward, smiling, and said, "Yes sir, Captain Barnes, when I was home [Barnes was unaware that the new recruit was also from Clarksdale] last weekend, I saw your daddy, and I promised him I'd be sure to take good care of you." Unlike Betty, this was one new recruit who had brought much of his hometown with him.

Cherry Point was mostly "just killing time" while waiting for her orders, but Betty has one singular memory concerning a double date. The other girl's date was a good-looking Marine pilot who drove a flashy red convertible. His name was Tyrone Power. Betty never saw that pilot again—except a few years later on the big silver screen.

Betty's orders arrived. She was to report for duty at naval air station at North Island, California, near San Diego, a few miles north of the Mexican border. This was the major continental US naval base supporting operating forces in the Pacific. She was thrilled. San Diego was a dream assignment in "the golden state," two thousand miles from Mississippi. California had high mountains, great beaches, San Francisco, Los Angeles, Hollywood, and was situated right next to Mexico. But first, Betty took two weeks of her annual leave and headed home to Clarksdale. Her first priority was a car of her own, and now with a regular paycheck, she could afford to buy one. She found a used green Chevy coupe (there were no new cars available in the middle of the war). When she heard that Richard Taylor, a friend from Ole Miss and a newly commissioned Marine pilot home on leave, also had orders for California, she called to see if he wanted a ride. He did.

Mid-July was a miserable, "hot as hinges" time to be making the long trip on Route 66, across six states filled with farmland, oil fields, desert, and mountains in temperatures over one hundred degrees. Adding to their misery, the car had no air conditioning. Betty remembers they felt honor bound to follow regulations: "The uniform of the day when traveling was the wool winter uniform and, like idiots, (or new second lieutenants) that's what we wore." The unhappy travelers had eight flat tires before they reached Oklahoma City, and when they arrived, they headed directly for the ra-

tion board. Rubber, an essential war material, was severely rationed, and even though herculean efforts to perfect
production of synthetic rubber were beginning to pay off,
most of the world's natural rubber producing areas were in
Southeast Asia and controlled by the Japanese. But the officials at the ration board in Oklahoma City must have believed the two newly commissioned Marine officers heading
for their first tour of duty were essential to the war effort—
or maybe the board functionaries had a soft spot for two
stranded second lieutenants. Betty received permission to
buy four new tires.

Spelling each other, with one driving while the other
slept—and with no more flats—Betty and Richard traveled
the remaining fifteen hundred miles to California in two
days. When they reached El Toro, Richard got out. Betty
then drove eighty miles to San Diego, took the ferry across
the bay to North Island, and reported for duty.

She was made a battalion communication officer, responsible for the maintenance manuals airplane mechan-
ics followed when repairing and refurbishing fighter planes
brought back to San Diego from the Pacific war zone. A
standing order required that all planes serving in combat
must regularly undergo a major overhaul, involving parts
replacement, repairs, refurbishing, and new paint. An air-
craft carrier loaded with planes, mostly Corsairs, pulled into
San Diego harbor about once a week. Betty admits that she
found "overseeing maintenance manuals was not much of
a challenge, kind of like a glorified librarian." But this was
her assignment, her first responsibility in the Corps, and she
resolved to do the best job possible.

Six to eight Marines were directly under her command.
All were women except for a top sergeant in the regular
Marines, who ran the office until Betty, a commissioned

officer, was assigned. The sergeant had been wounded in the battle at Guadalcanal the year before and reassigned to non-combatant duty stateside. Betty, learning of his history, figured this man would likely resent a woman—any woman—taking over his job and giving him orders. Before opening the office door on the first morning of her new assignment, Betty paused, took a deep breath, pulled herself up to her full five foot four height, squared her shoulders, and prepared herself to "put all the cards on the table." Walking in, Betty introduced herself and invited the sergeant to sit down and have a cup of coffee with her. Once the coffee was poured, she swallowed hard. "I know you don't like the idea of a woman in charge, but you have to give me some credit, I chose the best service. You have the reputation of running things right—doing a good job. Here's the deal. I want you to continue to run the office as you see fit. Get things done right, and I'll sign everything you put on my desk. But, if you foul up, I'm going to get your neck." From that very first day, things ran smoothly.

This may be one of those tricks of memory. A letter she sent home at the time indicates that things were not quite as "well run" as she remembered: "I have been working like the very devil on this new job. The publications were, & still are, in a complete mess, and I haven't enough room nor help to set things up as I would like. Then too, it is my first administrative job & I feel very green. I haven't had much experience at being an office executive, but guess I'll learn." But although Betty may have lacked prior administrative experience, she had self-confidence, an appreciation for the other person's feelings, and her own good sense. As a newly-minted lieutenant, she took command, defused a potentially explosive situation, and gained cooperation and respect from an experienced veteran. Betty recalls that she and the sergeant became good friends. In the years to come, in increasingly challenging and difficult situations, others would observe that Betty Bobo Pearson was a natural born leader.

She was smitten with California, with its mountains, valleys, ocean, and beaches, so very different from the flatlands around Clarksdale. She was eager to share the wonders of her new surroundings with her parents—particularly her father, owing to his strong identity with and love of his native soil. An excerpt from a letter home describes Betty's flight up to El Toro, where her unit was soon to be transferred:

> This is really pretty country to fly over. Taking off, we circle North Island and head up over San Diego . . . [she drew a map so her parents could visualize the area]. The Bay that extends about nine miles between Point Loma and San Diego is the most ideal harbor in the world. We follow the ocean up about 80 miles then swing inland across a low range of mountains. El Toro is between this and a farther range of mountains, right in the citrus district. The groves make perfect patterns of polka dots from the air. The taller mountains are snow-topped and from the air over El Toro you can see mountains to the east and west, the ocean beyond the western hills.

A few months after she wrote this letter, Betty was charged with what she remembers as the most "challenging and interesting job" she had during her entire stint in the Marine Corps. Her battalion was to be transferred to the two huge hangers at El Toro, and Betty was ordered to supervise the development of a master plan for the battalion's transfer from their present situation on North Island. Figuring out the exact placement of every piece of equipment to be moved—with some to be set in concrete—was a major, and to Betty, a daunting task. "Why they gave me the job, I will never know. It was hard, but plenty of math and mechanical drawing, so I was happy. It was interesting, and after it was over I felt good about it."

She was given a hanger wall, twenty feet tall and approximately thirty feet long, with scaffolding running the whole length, on which she could stand. Climbing up and down the scaffolding, Betty was to draw to scale the floor plan of their new base of operation, placing everything that had to be moved within an inch of where it was to be placed in the hangers at El Toro. "The desks and filing cabinets weren't too hard, but the other stuff was really tough—it took a long time," she recalls. Each department was responsible for giving Betty a sketch to scale of the placement of their equipment. She studied these and double-checked with the department heads when she had questions. Together with two enlisted people under her command, she applied long strips of tape and spray painted the lines of the plan with an airbrush she taught herself to use. "It was a huge responsibility and I was so scared that [when we got to El Toro] one of these things would come through a door and everything would foul out. But they didn't." The battalion was relocated without incident.

But it was not all work for the young, attractive, fun-loving second lieutenant from Mississippi. Her free time was chock full of good times. In another letter home Betty wrote:

> Last week was one of the worst I've ever spent. We got up every morning at 5:30 and didn't get back to WOQ (women officers' quarters) until 6. There was something on every night and we never got to bed before one in the morning. Richard [her cross-country traveling friend] came down Saturday and we stayed out until three danc-

ing, then went to Tijuana, Mexico for the horse races and bull fights. It was a wonderful weekend. But of course I was dead tired. Luckily Monday was my day off and I was still asleep when the others came in at 6 that evening. Tuesday and Wednesday we had baseball practice until 8 or 8:30. They are letting officers play in the league now. Lt. Strong is pitching, Gee Wright plays short center field, & I'm playing short stop. We're getting a darn good team together. The rec. dept is getting us uniforms. Richard is coming down again Saturday. Sunday evening we are going to La Jolla (to Capt. Curtis's house) and will barbeque steaks on the patio.

Betty's natural leadership capabilities shone. She was named recreation officer for the women Marines in her battalion. The two major sports were bowling (she'd never in her life picked up a bowling ball, but the battalion included a lot of enlisted women from the Midwest who were good bowlers) and softball, a sport Betty loved. Competition was fierce in the San Diego league, which consisted of twelve softball teams made up of Navy and Marine women serving in the southern California area. The year Betty was recreational officer, her team won the league championship and took tremendous pride and pleasure in wearing their snazzy khaki golf-type jackets with "1944 Champions—Naval Division 11," emblazoned across their backs. Additionally, Betty coached a women's rifle team in a full course of instruction in the fundamentals of rifle care and the firing of the weapons on the range. Having hunted with her father prior to entering the Corps, she was familiar and comfortable with guns.

In another letter home she wrote that she couldn't say much about her work, but that she was very happy working on a gigantic blueprint. She asked her mother to send her record collection. Many of the records in the collection were those she and Flossie bought in the shop in Jackson during their freshman year at Millsaps. She also asked her mother to have some calling cards made for her. Although a tomboy at heart, Betty knew and appreciated the importance of social grace; when mingling with top brass, she obviously wanted to display her familiarity and comfort with customary etiquette. Her instructions were: "Ladies' size without trim and no fancy letter style, everything written out in full—name in center and title in lower right corner." To be sure her mother understood her exact specifications, Betty drew a picture:

---

### ERIE ELIZABETH BOBO


SECOND LIEUTENANT
UNITED STATES MARINE CORPS RESERVE

---

A few lines later she allowed that "things are really going to be fouled up with Richard and a Lt. Creech, both here waiting to be shipped out, and [both] wanting weekend dates." Betty's life was full. She considered selling her car and plotted with friends to rent a two-bedroom apartment on the ocean when they got to El Toro. "Six of us will go together so it won't be too expensive. We will live on the base and use the apartment for weekends, dinners, evenings, etc. . . . It will be wonderful to have a place for poker games, just quiet evenings away from camp, or if any of us wants to have someone for dinner or cocktails. And then if anyone's family comes out, we'll have a place for them to stay."

Betty sold her car, moved to El Toro, and continued her responsibilities as battalion communications officer. The apartment was never rented, but her weekends were filled with adventure and good times. Her favorite spot to hang out in her free time was the "ready room," where the pilots waited to be called out for a flight. Theirs was a relaxed, easy camaraderie, playing Acey Ducey, "sort of an 'our gang' thing, not individual dates." Betty has glowing memories of flying all around the state with pilots returned from combat in the Pacific who were putting engine time on planes before being sent back overseas. "When not in the ready room, I might get a call, 'Bo, can you get away to fly up to San Francisco for the weekend?' All of my friends in the Marines called me Bo . . . and I would always respond, 'Sure, I'll find a way.' They'd fly here and yonder. Great fun—a wonderful break from boring base routines."

Betty flew home to Clarksdale twice while stationed in California. "It was almost impossible to get a reservation on a commercial airline, unless you were a Senator or somebody," she said, so she flew home on military planes. "The disadvantage was that you always had to check out a parachute. You couldn't fly in a military plane without a parachute. You had to check the parachute out and take it with you—it was your responsibility to bring it all the way back. Those things are heavy as lead . . . but at that age who cares. . . . I would leave San Diego or El Toro and maybe get as far as El Paso and have to spend the night there . . . then get up and go out to the air base the next morning to go somewhere [else along the way] finally ending up in Memphis." Her parents met her there to take her home to Clarksdale.

While in California, Betty's two best friends were Ginny (Captain Virginia Strong) and Gee (Eugenia Wright), another second lieutenant. One spring day, after the three transferred to El Toro, Gee and Betty took a two-week leave and went to Arizona. Gee, a wealthy girl from Delaware, had spent most summers with her family at a dude ranch in Arizona, where she owned a horse. Betty and Gee rode horses for two weeks and had such a "fabulous" time that at the end of their leave, they put Gee's horse in a trailer and took it back to California to stable it near their base.

After Arizona, the idea of an ocean-side apartment on the beach lost out to horseback riding in the mountains. Ginny and Betty rented horses, and together with Gee, explored the foothills of the Santa Ana Mountains, where there were ideal locations for weekend campouts. Betty remembers, "It was really an interesting time. We would take the horses and ride up in the hills and saw all those farms that had been confiscated from the Japanese. They'd just be boarded up, grown over." The mountains were rugged and beautiful. Riding through an avocado grove—where they had been told they could pick up anything that had fallen on the ground—the three friends gorged on the fruit. If they were spending the night, they took two cars. One, packed with with a case of beer, food, a tent, and sleeping bags, was parked where they wanted to camp. They drove the second car back to the horses, then rode up to their spot. Betty remembers, "I loved it. I loved the climate. I loved everything about California."

An officer in Betty's El Toro unit, who had been a set designer in Hollywood, asked her and some friends to go to the horse races at Santa Anita. When they were ushered to her host's box, Betty took one of the end seats. In the seat next to her in the adjacent box sat Cary Grant, the debonair matinee idol. He charmed the young lieutenant by asking all kinds of questions about her experience as a Marine. Dazzled, she said she would never forget the afternoon—but she remembered nothing about the horserace.

Always wanting to get the most out of anything she did, Betty bought a quarter horse named Jigger. "He was big, really too tall a horse for anybody as short as I am, and really fast. Jigger ran away with me at the beginning of every ride, until I could rein him in. Then he'd be fine." A man who worked at the stable where Betty boarded Jigger was convinced Betty's horse could win quarter horse races. Although she was not interested in racing, the fellow talked her into clocking Jigger's speed for a quarter of a mile. One sunny Saturday afternoon Gee, Ginny, Betty, and the man from the stable climbed into a van and trailered Jigger to a nearby track. It was a long straight run, with stands in the middle where the stable man stood with his stopwatch. Betty led her horse up the track and, as soon as she mounted, Jigger took off, racing past the stands at break-neck speed. Recounting the incident Betty said, "At the end of the track, I pulled hard, really hard, on the reins to turn him around, but Jigger, feeling the freedom of galloping full speed, raced straight ahead, jumped the fence at the edge of the park, and kept going. Thank goodness, it was a field with solid ground, not a chasm. It took me forever to stop him. He loved to run as hard as he could run." The man from the stable was ecstatic, insisting she had to race Jigger. Betty said, "Fine, but you'll have to find another jockey."

On August 15, 1945, the Japanese surrendered. On September 2, 1945, aboard the USS *Missouri* in Tokyo Bay, Japan formally signed the official documents of surrender, bringing the hostilities of World War II to a close. The war was over. It was the passing of an era. For the past four years, every US service man and woman, and every US civilian had been dedicated to the defeat of the Axis powers and the preservation of freedom. "We all were convinced of the rightness of the cause," Betty declares. Now the cause was won. It was time to go home. Betty mustered out of the Marine Corps Reserve, packed her bags, sold Jigger, and headed back to Mississippi to think things over before deciding what to do with the rest of her life.

# A New Beginning

*When you find a heart-mate, appreciate it all the way. . . .*
—Betty Bobo Pearson

It was August 1945, and the war was over. Betty received her discharge from active duty later that fall, and she toyed with the idea of using the GI bill to attend graduate school at the University of California, Berkeley. She had no idea what type of degree to pursue. Her earlier interest in journalism had waned, and it was not until years later, while digging in her renowned garden at her home, Rainbow Plantation, that she had second thoughts about graduate studies: "I never knew [when I had the opportunity for graduate school] that I was interested in gardens. . . . I would have loved to have gone back to get my degree in landscape design. That's what I should have done. But then I didn't know that was what I was that interested in, and by the time I knew, it was too late."

Betty loved California. It offered so much—the mountains, the seashore, an explosion of things to do and see—but she knew it was time to leave. It would never again be the same as it was during the war. Her good friends were spreading out across the nation, heading for home, so she, too, decided to head for home. She returned to live for a while in her parents' big house in Clarksdale, where they had moved while Betty was in college. Her brother, Bob, recently discharged after his service in the Pacific, was also back home, planning to go into business with his father. Betty and Bob's father wanted both of his children to remain close by forever and came up with a scheme to keep his daughter near him, too.

Betty's father knew the avalanche of returning veterans, eager to get on with their lives, created an outstanding business opportunity: all of those returning soldiers would be wanting "good home cooking." Seeing a way to keep his independent-minded daughter "down on the farm," he offered her a chance to get in on the ground floor of the up-and-coming poultry industry. She could start her own business out at Bobo, raising and selling chickens. Betty, not really knowing what she wanted to do with her life, liked the idea. She liked the challenge of starting her own business. She would be her own boss and run her own enterprise, a rare opportunity for a woman in the 1940s, when practically the only career options for an educated, single women were nursing or teaching. She also liked the idea of daily contact with Big Mama, her beloved grandmother.

That spring, Betty started her own little business. She hired three women to slaughter and dress small, succulent broilers, which she then sold fresh to the grocers and restaurateurs in the area, as well as door-to-door to her neighbors. In those years, most families did not eat chicken, unless they raised the birds in their own back yards, so chicken was a rare item in grocery stores and restaurants. Betty's chicken enterprise flourished, and then this budding entrepreneur recognized an additional opportunity. Later that spring, she bought and raised a brood of poults (baby turkeys) to be served at Thanksgiving dinners the following November. When November arrived, she sold every one.

Betty was glad to be home in the comfort and security

of Clarksdale, among family, friends and familiar places. Superficially, much was the same as when she had left two years earlier, she recalled, "The Mississippi Delta back then, more than it is now, was just one big community. If you went to high school in Clarksdale, you knew everybody your age in Greenwood, Rosedale and Cleveland—you saw everybody at parties and dances. When we were juniors and seniors in high school we drove sixty or seventy miles to a dance." After the war, most of the young folk in Betty's old Delta crowd were married and starting families. And yet, eager to re-establish connections, they still thought nothing of driving sixty or seventy miles for a party.

It didn't take long for Betty to relax into the comfortable pace of her old social network. The following summer she spent most of her time not dating, but enjoying movies, parties, going out to dinner, sandbar picnics, and driving to Memphis as part of a compatible foursome. The arrangement had much in common with the Marine "our gang" atmosphere of her social life in Californian. Betty enjoyed doing things with her good friend Mary Martha Presley and two of the unattached men from their old crowd, George "Pippy" McFalls and Bill Pearson. Betty and Bill had known each other since the two of them were in a wedding when they were both four years old, when Bill was ring bearer and Betty was a flower girl. They were the same age, they belonged to the same social set, and they shared many of the same interests, but they had never dated.

At the end of the war, Bill was stationed in Hawaii as an Army pilot, in no particular hurry for his return to civilian life. When he received his discharge, he thought he would probably go to law school at Yale or North Carolina and then practice law, or maybe earn a PhD and teach at the college level. He never intended to be a Delta planter. The sudden death of his uncle, who managed the family plantation a few miles outside of Sumner, Mississippi, changed all that.

In late October of 1945, when he received word of his uncle's heart attack, Bill was granted an emergency leave from active duty, with orders to return to Hawaii in early January. Once he was home, it did not take long for Bill to realize he could not return to the Army. The war was over, and his family needed him. Bill contacted his good friend William (Billy) Wynn, a lawyer in Greenville, Mississippi, who had connections in Washington and represented the Delta Council, an organization of cotton growers. A native son of the Mississippi Delta, Bill knew that land creates privilege, and that privilege gives access to power. Wynn contacted Mississippi Senator James Eastland, and Bill Pearson received a discharge from the Army. Bill's life course was set. Family loyalty ran strong and his dreams of law school vanished. He remained in Mississippi to manage his family's twenty-six hundred acre plantation. Remembering those days, he said, "It just became incumbent on me to run the farm, to do the farming." He started working for his mother.

As he revised his personal aspirations and settled into his new life, Bill spent most of his free time with three old friends, enjoying the easy-going camaraderie they had. One afternoon, towards the end of the following summer, Bill called Betty to ask if she was free for dinner that night. Following their customary routine, Betty responded, "I am. I'll call Mary Martha to see if she is."

"No, don't call Mary Martha, I'm asking you."

That evening, Betty Bobo and Bill Pearson had their first real date—just the two of them. Thinking back, Betty said, "I'll never forget how adorable he was. He was the funniest thing. I just laughed the whole time. He was just so full of himself."

After dinner Bill drove Betty home and walked her to the door. As they told each other goodnight, he said, "Let's get married." Stunned, Betty responded, "Get married! I don't know you well enough to marry you." "Oh, well, OK," Bill said. He shrugged his shoulders, turned around, walked back to his car, and drove away.

Over the summer, Bill had begun to realize his feelings toward Betty were more than casual. She was smart, fun loving, energetic, ambitious, and open-minded. She was also a levelheaded, good-looking woman, with whom he shared values and interests. He always knew Betty was special, but he was feeling something more, much more—he was in love. He wanted to marry Betty Bobo. She would make the perfect partner, a great companion, a wonderful mother—an ideal wife.

Betty didn't close her eyes that night. Her heart, her mind, her whole being churned with questions, doubts, desires, memories, hopes, and dreams. Get married? Most of her friends were already married, it was probably time. She was twenty-four years old. Bill was so smart, so accomplished. Friends claimed he was the smartest man they knew. She and Bill enjoyed doing the same things, liked the same people, laughed at the same jokes. Betty could think of no better man than Bill Pearson. They shared the same values. Both of them had experienced and appreciated the world beyond the Delta, yet both loved their native land—they talked often of ways to make it better.

Did she love him? Probably. He was great to be with. He was good-looking, and even-tempered and balanced in his ways. Betty had always wanted to live in the country and have her own place. "Rainbow," she mused, what a nice name. Towards morning she began to realize that she and Bill could build a wonderful life together. Their children would have the life she knew and loved, rooted in land and family. Bill's proposal made sense. The more Betty thought about marrying Bill, the more it seemed like a good idea— an extremely good idea. She came to a decision, "Oh well, hmm. . . . Yeah." Betty Bobo wanted to marry Bill Pearson.

That evening Betty's parents were having a party to which Bill was invited. The guests arrived and were clustered in conversation or milling around the long dining table laden with the usual mounds of Delta party food: small biscuits stuffed with country ham, cucumber canapés, a huge cut glass bowl of pickled shrimp. Betty pulled Bill aside. "Bill, do you know what we were talking about last night?"

Lifting an eyebrow and tilting his head, enjoying the chance for a good tease, he said, "We talked about a lot of things last night."

"Bill, no, you know."

"No, what do you mean?"

Bill swore that he made Betty ask him to marry her before he finally asked, "You mean you know me well enough?" To which she promptly responded, "Yeah, I know you well enough."

The next day, eager to tell Big Mama her news, Betty phoned to make sure her grandmother would be home when she drove out to Bobo that afternoon. "Oh, Honey, I'm coming to town today, so I can see you up there," Big Mama said. "Well," Betty responded, "come by Mother's house, as I have something to tell you."

Betty, Lenora, and Bill were sitting in the living room of her parents' home when Big Mama appeared at the door, dressed as any "proper" lady going to town in 1946 would be. She wore a small brimmed, pillbox hat, a long-sleeved, smartly tailored navy blue dress, white gloves, nylon stockings and sensible two-inch heeled pumps. Betty jumped up and hurried over to give her a hug. "Big Mama, I wanted to tell you before anyone else knew about it. Bill and I are getting married."

Big Mama turned, looked at Bill. "Young man do you drink?" Bill answered, "Well, Ma'am, sometimes."

With that, Big Mama locked eyes with him, pulled off her hat, and hurled it backhanded, as if she were throwing a Frisbee. The flat little pillbox sailed the length of the living room—a good twenty-five feet—hit the fireplace mantel and dropped to the floor. Her voice pierced the air: "Well, I'll tell you one thing, young man. You're not good enough for her." Laughing, Bill picked up the hat and handed it to Big Mama. "Well, Miss Bessie, I certainly can agree with you on that."

Later, remembering that day, Betty said, "I knew that Big Mama didn't want me to marry anybody. I think, I really think, I was her favorite grandchild. Nobody would be good enough for me."

A few days later Bill told Betty he had to go to town to talk with her father. Betty asked, "Why?"

"I have to ask him for your hand in marriage."

"You don't have to do that."

"Well, I certainly do."

Bob Bobo's daughter may have served in the United States Marines for two years, but she was still her daddy's little girl. Bill Pearson may have been an Army pilot throughout World War II, but he was still a Southern gentleman.

The young couple wanted to get married right away—but they waited. It was important, absolutely essential to Lenora, that her only daughter be married in the First Methodist Church of Clarksdale. The church was undergoing renovations and would not be available until February, necessitating a delay of four or five months. In early October, Betty and Bill announced their engagement. When the invitations were sent, Betty said her parents invited "everyone in kingdom come."

Even in normal times, a wedding between a Bobo and a Pearson, two of "the first families" of the Mississippi Delta, would occasion a commanding social flurry. But this was the first wedding since the war had ended, the first opportunity to honor someone and entertain in style. During the following three months, Betty and Bill's engagement was celebrated by "way over a hundred parties." Many days, Betty would be the honoree at a luncheon, then attend an afternoon tea, which was followed by a party for the young couple that night. She says of that period, "Exhausting. I lost a lot of weight."

But it was not all parties and wedding plans that fall. Betty's growing business had a large number of orders for Thanksgiving turkeys, and Bill stepped in to help with deliveries. Often when he made a call, the customer would take the turkey, look Bill over, and remark, "Ah, so you're the one she's going to marry."

So soon after the war, many in Betty and Bill's social set confronted a major problem: finding a fitting wedding present for the soon-to-be married couple. The gift shop in Clarksdale had little to offer, so Betty's father went scouting. He found a set of bone china somewhere, bought the whole set, and brought it back to Clarksdale to be resold in the shop where Betty was registered. Bob Bobo made certain that his daughter would always be able to set a proper table.

Arrangements for the wedding ceremony were of equal concern to Lenora, the mother of the bride. Betty's gown, the dresses for the bridesmaids, the flowers, the music, the reception were matters of intense interest for her. All Betty wanted was to marry Bill; she had no interest in such details. As a young girl, climbing trees, sailing, softball, and tennis were her passions—never fashion or concerns about what to wear. She liked the Marine regulation requiring a dress uniform for all social occasions. Betty said, "It was my mother's wedding. She asked things like, 'Now what color do you want the bridesmaids' dresses to be?' And I would respond, 'I don't care what color. You pick the color, Mama.' I really didn't care." Lenora came up with the answer. Betty's young first cousin, four-year-old Emily Jean Corley, was to be the flower girl and wear a copy of the yellow dress Betty wore when she was a flower girl and Bill the ring bearer in the 1925 wedding. The bridesmaids' dresses would be yellow. But what about the all-important dress? Betty said, "Mama was very interested in what kind of gown I was going to wear. I was not very interested in what kind of gown I was going to wear. I can't remember. We came up with something. I think she was happy."

When the February wedding date finally arrived, the workmen were behind schedule and had not refinished the church floors. There were no pews in the sanctuary. Betty's father again stepped in, ordering that the pews be put back in the church and temporarily screwed down for the ceremony. He did not want any of his guests stumbling in their formal attire. One of those guests, a young friend of the couple who was still in high school, remembers Bill and Betty's wedding as "all candles and flowers."

As an usher, in his stiff white shirt and black tail coat, seated a late arrival, the organist began to play Mendelssohn's "Wedding March," the bridesmaids, dressed in billowing pale yellow skirts, glided down the center aisle. Lenora was very happy. Betty said the only decision she made about the wedding arrangements was made in deference to her grandmother. "Big Mama didn't approve of drinking, so I said only punch at the reception. Since it was before the days of open bars at weddings, it went okay—after Bill and I left and my parents went to bed, Bob opened the liquor closet, and people in the wedding had a great party."

On the evening of February 12, 1947, standing on unfinished floors in the First United Methodist Church of Clarksdale, Mississippi, Erie Elizabeth Bobo and William Wallace Pearson exchanged their marriage vows, creating a union that, at the time of this writing, is in its sixty-ninth year. Betty married her soul mate, her best friend, a supportive partner, a fun companion. With compatible intelligence, shared values, and similar cultural roots, Bill was a genuinely good man who, in the coming years and in his quiet way, stood behind Betty in solid support as she stepped into the public arena filled with virulent controversy that created heart-breaking strife among beloved members of her family.

# Under the Rainbow

*The plantation mistress was the most important personage
about the home, the presence that pervaded . . . the centre of
all that life, the queen of the realm . . . which bound all the
rest of the structure and gave it strength and beauty.*
—Thomas Nelson Page (1893)

When the newlyweds, both twenty-four years old, started
their life at Rainbow, Bill knew little—and Betty knew nothing at all—about raising cotton. Rainbow Plantation consisted of twenty-six hundred acres, with forty tenant houses
and about one hundred black tenants, three tractors, and
thirty or so mules. The young couple planned and plotted
for months before their move. They had set their minds and
hearts on modernizing the place, mechanizing the labor,
educating the workers, improving workers' housing, beating
the boll weevil, destroying the tobacco budworms, making a
good living, and creating an inviting, attractive home where
everyone felt welcome. It was a time of major transition
for cotton farming, and there were many things that were
wrong at Rainbow. Raising cotton had always been very labor intensive, with hoeing and picking done by hand, and
production was severely affected during World War II, when
most of the labor left the South. Soon after the war, when Bill
arrived to manage Rainbow, there were about forty tenant/
sharecropper families, mostly old folks and single women,
living on the plantation. Although some of the tenants "who

didn't trust a twenty-four-year-old boy to run things" left, this did not bother Bill. Mechanical cotton pickers were being introduced to the market, and he wanted to mechanize as quickly as possible.

For several months immediately after the wedding, the young couple lived with Bill's grandmother, "Mawmaw," who lived in a big white house directly across the street from the Delta Inn in Sumner. The inn, an imposing three-story brick building with white columns in front, was built to accommodate traveling salesmen after the railroad came to the Delta. Bill came home every day to have lunch with Betty, and occasionally they would go across to the Delta Inn to eat. Meals were served at long tables, and one sat where there was a space.

On one occasion they sat at a table with a number of men who were working on the natural gas line being put in near Sumner. One of the men overhearing the name Bobo in the Pearsons' conversation, leaned over and said, "Excuse me, but I heard you mention Bobo, and I wonder if you know the Bobo family in Clarksdale?" Betty nodded, and he went on to say,

> I grew up in Glendora, and in the early twenties the train coming through town every afternoon was a big event. All of the little boys went down to the station to see the engine and wave at the engineer. One day when I was eight or ten years old, there was a terrible wreck—a train hit a car as it was crossing the track, and the amazing thing was a little baby in the car was thrown out onto the cowcatcher of the engine, and when the train finally stopped the baby rolled off into the ditch. I ran down and picked the baby up and took it back to the lady who was driving the car, who was now screaming hysterically, "My baby, where is my baby?"

I learned that the family involved were the Bobos from Clarksdale, but I never knew whether the baby was a boy or a girl, or what happened to it. Do you know anything about it?

Awed to meet the boy, now man, she had heard about all of her life, Betty stood up, held out her hand, and said, "Thank you very much for taking me back to my mother."

Betty and Bill moved from Mawmaw's house out to Rainbow in the early spring. The main farmhouse on the plantation, built in 1914, had four rooms with a hall down the middle, a single-board exterior, un-insulated walls and floors, a lean-to for the kitchen, and another lean-to for the bathroom. It was quite a change from Betty's parents' house in Clarksdale and Mawmaw's house in Sumner.

The plantation had not always been called Rainbow. When Bill's grandfather, William Marion Simpson, and another landowner in the area, J. J. Webb, bought the land together in 1918, the plantation was known as Esum, the name of the whistle-stop located on the land. Bill's grandmother hated the name Esum. One day about two years later, when Bill's father, Wally, who was a pilot during World War I, flew over the plantation, he noticed the fields looked like a rainbow as they curved around an old ox-bow lake called Staten Brake. Bill's grandmother was delighted with this image and insisted on re-naming their land Rainbow Plantation. Betty found Rainbow a perfect name for the place where she and Bill would realize their dream.

Building that dream was not easy. In their first year at Rainbow the crop failed. Spring planting had gone well, and by mid-summer the maturing plants were flourishing, so Betty and Bill decided to take a few weeks of vacation on the Gulf Coast before it was time to pick the cotton. They returned home to find the grass in the fields higher than the shriveled, dying cotton plants. Blight, a Delta farmer's scourge, had struck. There was no redeemable cotton. Bill took control of Rainbow the next year. Crop management, the young couples' livelihood, was his responsibility, and he was determined to combat and find answers to such devastation. Seeking help from the experts, he befriended the research scientists at the Stoneville Agricultural Experiment Station (a resource other farmers in the area seemed to ignore), and he read every agricultural textbook he could find.

After this first-year disaster, Bill, short of cash, rented a third of the place out for two years, fired the white overseer, and picked the best black worker on the farm to replace the fired man. Such a replacement was unique in that time, but a wise decision. Dook Petty worked for the Pearsons for the next thirty years. Then he retired on Social Security. Dook's success was the genesis of an enlightened management style Bill continued to develop over subsequent years of farming. Three years after that disastrous first year, Bill felt confident enough to restore Rainbow to its original size, and he planted and harvested all of his land.

Rainbow Plantation remained the same size for the next forty-five years and, over time, developed a reputation as a fine place to work. Bill was never interested in getting bigger by acquiring more land; he only wanted to do better, do the very best that was possible with what they had. It took five years before Rainbow started making money, and over the following decades (they eventually sold the plantation in 1991), Bill broke every established rule for raising cotton in the Delta. To replace laborers with hoes, he put geese in the fields for grass control and experimented with flame cultivation by actually burning out the weeds and grass. The first in the area to hire an entomological consultant, Bill tested multiple methods of crop control and enhancement, and he was pleased to watch his yearly yields increase and eventually double. In order to compare the results of different methods and products, in a single year he divided his land into four separate fields and planted and treated each field differently. Bill tried anything and everything to improve his annual yield—even political suasion in the nation's capitol.

In the 1950s, cotton production was controlled by government allotment. A farmer could plant only so many acres in evenly spaced rows. When Bill discovered that he could improve his yield by skip-row planting—planting two rows of cotton and skipping a row—it was obvious to him that the government rules requiring even row planting should be changed. He wrote letters to the Department of Agriculture explaining his success with the new method. He never received a response. The rules did not change. After several years of growing frustration, Bill realized letters would not change the system. He would have to go to Washington and personally explain the problem. He made an appointment with Senator Eastland and went to Washington. Later Bill said, "I must have bored the Senator to death. I just preached and preached. I'd done skip row myself for two years and had such good luck with it, I was shocked [that nothing was being done to change the regulations]. I told him the whole story and he didn't say anything."

Two years later, in the spring of 1962, Bill, Betty, and their daughter, Erie, went to Washington to show Erie the nation's Capitol. Bill went by Senator Eastland's office to get tickets to the White House. His secretary said, "The senator wants to see you." Bill said, "I don't want to bother the senator, I just want tickets to the White House." "No, no you have to go in to see the senator," replied the secretary.

Bill walked into Eastland's office, and the senator said,

"Boy, I got the law for you. Two and one is going to be legal this year." His supposition confirmed, Bill thanked the senator. Success growing cotton depended on cultivating the politicians, as well as the land. "I was no longer penalized," Bill recalled. The measurement of the rows actually supporting cotton plants would determine the size of his allotment, not the measurement of the field in which the cotton was planted.

During the 1980s, Bill founded the annual Rainbow seminars to bring people from all over the world to the plantation to discuss agricultural methods and learn more about raising cotton. In 1983, he received the *Cotton Grower* achievement award. Those who nominated him said Bill Pearson "conducts so many on-farm trials that his Rainbow Plantation has . . . the characteristics of a research farm."

Even though Bill Pearson led the field in mechanization, experimentation, and innovation of cotton farming in the Delta, he wanted to run a "happy ship." He cared about his workers and took pains to develop their skills, build their competence, and give them self-confidence. When a thing was not done well, or there was a problem, rather than criticize, Bill customarily claimed he had not made his instructions clear. He wanted his workers to be more independent and to accept responsibility for their own lives, but it was an uphill battle. Everyone—black and white—expected the plantation owner to take care of his people.

The success of the crop was Bill's responsibility and provided Rainbow's livelihood, yet Rainbow was much more. As mistress of Rainbow, that "so much more" was largely Betty's responsibility. Thomas Nelson Page's words, quoted at the beginning of this chapter, were written in 1893, fifty-four years before Betty moved to Rainbow as a new bride. Although plantation life was changing, the expectations for the mistress were largely unchanged: She was to bring strength and beauty (many of Betty's friends would add the word "magic") to Rainbow.

The world beyond the Delta challenged traditional plantation culture, particularly attitudes surrounding two issues: the role of women outside the home, and the position and treatment of Negroes. Those two challenges were important to Betty and gave her a sense of purpose. Political, economic, and educational opportunities were expanding for women and for blacks in most other parts of the country. Betty made it clear that although she loved Rainbow and felt a true sense of responsibility and joy in her new role as mistress of the plantation, she did not agree with the Delta's deeply ingrained attitudes and practices—a pervasive ethos that shaped the lives of those around her.

One incident during her first year at Rainbow demonstrated how a cultural practice can become so habitual that individuals no longer give any thought to their actions. One November afternoon in 1947, Bill arrived home and casually mentioned to Betty that he had saved her the trouble of going to vote. He had voted for her when he was in town. Stunned, Betty said, "You did what?" In the all-male Mississippi political culture of the time, it was believed that when a husband voted for his wife, he was doing her a favor. Since women had no stake in the game, he saved his woman the trouble of going to the polls. Although Betty's independent spirit and keen sense of civic responsibility were assets Bill admired, he unconsciously adopted the well-established cultural practice. It would be the last time he voted for Betty.

Two years later, Bill solved another "political matter," and this time Betty was deeply grateful. Bill and Betty's daughter, Erie, the Pearsons' first and only child, was born in November 1949. The new mother could not have been happier, until one day the following spring when she opened her mail. The Korean War had begun, and Betty had received a notice recalling her to active duty. She said, "It scared me out of my mind. I had this little baby a couple of months old and I got this letter saying, *you are to put your affairs in order as you will be recalled to active duty within six months.* I told Bill, I was going over the hill, or something, but I was not leaving him and my baby." Betty was still in the reserves when she came home after the war, but she had never given a thought to any further military obligation, never considered that she could be recalled. Petrified, she had no idea what to do. Bill picked up the phone and once again called Billy Wynn, his lawyer friend in Greenville. Wynn in turn called Senator Eastland and explained the situation. A couple of weeks later a letter arrived, advising that an honorable discharge from the US Marine Reserves had been granted to Betty Bobo Pearson.

Little Erie's childhood at Rainbow was much the same as her mother's early years in the country at Bobo, except that Erie did not have a little brother, and her parents included her in many of their outings. For most folks in Mississippi, fall and football are synonymous. The Pearsons had season tickets for Ole Miss football and until the 1970s went to every game, whether played at Oxford or on the road. On game days in Oxford, their crowd did not head for the Grove—where most Rebel fans gathered, and which some said looked like a Confederate encampment—but parked instead in front of the engineering building, close to clean, accessible restrooms. A group of four or five couples from Clarksdale met to share an elaborate, carefully packed, tailgate picnic before heading into the stadium. On one such afternoon, Erie, about six or seven years old, wore a cute little navy blue, sailor-type dress with a white collar. The Pearsons' seats were close to the student cheering section, and Erie found the cheerleaders far more interesting than the football players. She asked her mother if she could go closer to watch. Betty said, "OK, Erie. You can go down to where they are, but don't get in their way. You know where we are and just stay right there so I can see you." Betty, caught up in the excitement of the game, "kind of forgot to watch where Erie was." Within a few minutes, the man behind her tapped her on the shoulder. "Isn't that your little girl over there on the bench with the football players?" Betty looked down to the near side of the field, and there sat little Erie on the players' bench, a spot of navy between the red jerseys of two huge players. She had climbed over the tall fence separating the stands and the field. She wanted to get closer to the cheerleaders, and once there, found a good place to sit. When Ole Miss made a touchdown, all the players on the bench stood up, went to the sideline, and cheered for the players coming back up the field. Erie, like a member of the team, stood with those on the bench, went to the sideline, and clapped along. What a day! What a game! Betty let Erie be until after the game, when one of the players lifted the little girl back over the fence into her mama's arms.

In fighting the enculturation of racial attitudes plaguing their society, both Pearsons wanted it understood that they judged and valued individuals for whom they were, not according to the color of their skin. They were gradually able to improve living conditions for their workers. They built new houses with electricity and indoor plumbing for those who worked at Rainbow. It was more difficult to change the culture of paternalism—not to mention the impossibility of changing the segregated society in which they lived.

As mistress of Rainbow, Betty relished her role supervising food preparation, housekeeping, homemaking, gardening, decorating, entertaining, social life, and her myriad relationships beyond Rainbow. Like the hub of a wheel, Betty held the center, responsible for the training (when needed), welfare, and health of the people she hired. She knew quality and insisted on things being done right.

In 1965, after the Pearsons had lived at Rainbow for fifteen years, Bill attended Harvard University's advanced management program for three months, leaving Betty responsible for the total management of Rainbow and making the crop. She orchestrated the logistics: which field to pick and when, getting in front of the rain, dealing with breakdowns at the gin, the death of a tractor driver, figuring the yields, deciding on a second picking, disking for weeds, anticipating the market, and paying the bills. It was harvest time, and she had oversight decisions to make every moment of every day. At 8:00 p.m., most every night, she fell into bed exhausted. Joe Busby, the man who ran the gin at the time, told Carolyn Webb about ginning operations when "Mr. Bill" was at Harvard. The pickers brought the cotton into the gin, and "Miss Betty drove up in that little yellow Mercedes station wagon to tell me, 'Joe, don't you turn the heat up on the cotton.' The drier the cotton gets, the smaller it gets." Joe added, "I'd see that little yellow car coming, I'd turn that heat down. I'd see that little yellow car drive off, I'd turn that heat up." The workers at Rainbow knew their business, and Betty Pearson made the crop. She was satisfied.

When Betty was asked to think back on her days at Rainbow, three women stood out in her memory: Sadie Tucker, Rosie Rollins, and Alma "Puddin" Bradford Tucker. When Bill and Betty moved to Rainbow, Walter Tucker, the general handyman and hostler in charge of the mules, was already there with Sadie, his wife. Sadie's charm and good-natured efficiency immediately captured Betty's heart. Betty could not have had a better teacher as she began to learn what was expected of a plantation mistress. When Erie was born, Sadie also became a wonderful baby nurse. Sadie didn't have any children of her own, and she and Betty both doted on the baby. Sadie and baby Erie were inseparable. They truly adored each other. Erie was eighteen months old when Sadie died, and Betty feels losing Sadie was a traumatic event for Erie.

After Sadie died, Rosie Rollins came to Rainbow. Betty described Rosie as a great cook with a wonderful sense of humor. In addition to serving tasty meals, Rosie contributed a great deal to the delightful ambience at Rainbow for over twenty years. During the early years, Bobbie Simms, the entomologist Bill hired to study the insects destroying the crops, and the three young boys working with him in the fields, came once a week for one of Rosie's substantial, noon-time dinners of meat and vegetables. Bill and Betty frequently entertained local friends or out of town visitors with a Rosie-prepared casual evening meal or formal sit-down dinner. Betty recalled,

One time in the middle years Bill and I were sitting at the dining room table having lunch, and Bill was worried. We'd had one of those years when everything bad happened— like it does farming cotton—the market was down, there wasn't enough money, we'd had a bad summer, and the crops were bad. Moaning and groaning about money, Bill was telling me I just had "to cut back." Rosie, going back and forth from the kitchen serving things, stopped at one point and said, "Well now, if times are that bad, I guess I'm going to have to quit workin' for you all." Bill quickly retorted, "Ah no, no Rosie, don't worry about that. We can pay you your salary. It's ok, I just want Betty to cut back." I was trying hard to calm her down, when she said, "No sir, I guess I'm just going to have to quit. My mama once told me, 'Honey don't you never work for no poor white folks.' And with that she goes, 'heh, heh, heh, heh, heh,' and walks back in the kitchen. We could hear her in there just howling about her joke."

Rosie was the first black person at Rainbow to register to vote. Bill and Betty tried to make it plain they wanted everybody on their place to vote, and asked that everybody go register. Nobody did. Frustrated, Betty wondered if they were not sure if she and Bill really meant it. So she figured, if she could get a couple of people registered, it would "kind of open the gate." She told Rosie, "If you'll go in to town to register, I'll go with you." Then, said Betty, "Rosie rolled her eyes and said, 'Well, all right if you want me to register to vote, I don't mind registering, but you white folks been voting all this time and I can't see that's done much good.'" To which Betty responded, "I can't see much good either."

"Rosie was a hoot. One of the funniest human beings I've ever known in my life," Betty recalled. When Rosie was getting to the end of being able to work, she wanted to retire on Social Security, but she wasn't sure how old she was. Betty asked her where she was born. Rosie said she was born somewhere down in southern Mississippi, but they couldn't find a birth certificate. Betty asked where she went to school. When Rosie told her, Betty got in touch with the school district in that area and asked if they could find records for Rosie. After some searching, they found Rosie had started school at a certain age in a certain year. So Betty figured Rosie was sixty-seven, but Rosie thought she was sixty-five. She said, "I ain't no sixty-seven, I'm sixty-five." Betty suggested that when Rosie registered to vote, "Let's just go with the proof we have and play like you're sixty-seven because we've got it in writing."

They went down to the courthouse to Mrs. Rodgers, the circuit clerk, and Betty walked in and said that they'd come because Rosie wanted to register to vote. Betty remembered, "Mrs. Rodgers look[ed] at me like she could cut my throat and asked if we had something to write with. Neither Rosie nor I had anything, so I told Mrs. Rodgers that we'd go buy a pen. We walked across the street to the drugstore, bought a pen, came back, and Rosie started filling out a form. When she got to the blank for her age, Rosie asked, 'Do you want me to put down that Social Security age or my real age?'" Betty adds, "At that point, I thought we were going to get kicked out before we got started," but Rosie did indeed get registered.

About six months after Sadie died, her husband, Walter, went to Betty and said, "I need to talk to you about something. . . . I know folks are going to say it is too soon, but Miss Betty, I can't live without a woman. I loved Sadie, I wish she was still alive, but she's not. I found this girl named Puddin that I love, and she wants to marry me, and she is with another man's child, and I just want to talk with you about it." Betty said, "If you want to marry her, and it will make you happy, don't worry about how long it's been." After Puddin's baby was born, Walter married her and adopted her baby, named Jean. Betty said, "He was as good with that child as he was with his and Puddin's four children." She marveled at how relaxed and open Walter was to the situation. He gave Jean his last name, and she felt secure in her family, but she also knew her real father (who was overseas in Korea when she was born) and later spent time with him.

When Walter asked Betty to give Puddin a chance to work

for her, Betty agreed: "Puddin came to work and we immediately hit it off." From that time on, Betty claimed Puddin as one of her best friends. "I adored Puddin from the beginning because we got along so well." Erie was then a three-year-old toddler, and Puddin had baby Jean, so Betty and Puddin reared their children together. In many ways, Betty treated Puddin like a little sister. She wanted to teach her as much as she could. Many years before, Betty taught her little brother to read before he started school; now it was Puddin's turn to become Betty's student. Betty recalled, "Puddin, next to Bill Pearson, has the world's best disposition. I'm not an easy person to get along with when I'm in the driver's seat. People who worked for me had to do things the right way. And so Puddin did things the way I wanted them done, and I believe that when she learned to do things well, she valued the fact and appreciated knowing how to do things the right way."

Betty was never sure when or if Puddin might be upset about something: "Puddin is so even-tempered . . . kept her own counsel, so it was hard to know. I don't think we ever had a cross word. During the Emmett Till trial and afterwards during the civil rights troubles, I had to ask Puddin her reactions. It was kind of hard to dig it out of her . . . how do you feel about this, what do you think about that?" Puddin kept her own counsel. Years later, she said, "Miss Betty often asked me to take her car and deliver a message about an NAACP meeting," usually in a black church. "I'd always take my gun, hid here, [she pointed to her bosom] 'cause I'd have to drive through some mean folks' property. In fact, whenever Miss Betty and I went some place together . . . everywhere she'd go, she wanted me to go . . . I'd always have my gun. She never knew I was carrying one. But she knew if she ever needed help, all she had to do was call one of the tractor drivers. They all toted guns." Puddin said that one time when Betty gave her a note to carry to a lady, "Mr. Bill told me to go one way and come back another, by a field where he and the tractor drivers were working. I was to blow my horn, so he'd know I was safe." Puddin didn't know if Bill knew she carried a gun; they never discussed it. But Puddin didn't think anyone would mess with Betty for "holding up for black folks. Miss Betty would just say [to white folks], 'you hate black folks but have them cooking for you and taking care of your children.' She had the guts to join the NAACP."

Walter was illiterate (Betty never took Walter to register to vote because she didn't want to get in a tussle about reading and writing), but when Puddin went, she was quick to tell the lady who offered to help, "I'll sign my own name." Puddin had a sixth or seventh grade education and realized the importance of education. Her son, James Tucker, remembers playing hooky when he was about ten years old. The principal called Rainbow to report his absence, and Betty went to the Tucker house. She found James playing outside, loaded him in her car, and took him back to school—much to James's embarrassment. Betty wanted to make sure the children at Rainbow got an education. In fact, the Pearsons paid for Jean Tucker, Puddin's first child, to go to the Catholic high school in Clarksdale, and sent her to a summer program at Yale. When Jean graduated from twelfth grade, she received a scholarship to Cornell, went to law school, and eventually became a lawyer.

Betty's daughter, Erie, now a grown woman with her own family, talked about growing up on Rainbow from an insider's point of view: "Mom always had projects, always active, directing everyone. She was the boss of everybody. Everyone looked to her, and she taught the workers [so much]. Word got around that working on Rainbow was a good thing. The whole culture [outside of Rainbow] was so patronizing—my grandmother Lenora was dismissive of Addie [her cook], and my dad's mom referred to the 'darkies, who smelled bad,' but my parents always offered dignity to a person. At Rainbow there was a qualitatively different relationship [between the blacks and whites]." Erie and Jean Tucker were best of friends, constantly together. When Erie outgrew the beautiful, handmade dresses her grandmother Lenora made for her, they went to Jean. The two girls were probably about eleven years old when their conversation turned to weddings and getting married. Erie told Jean, "You are going to be maid of honor in my wedding." Jean quickly replied, "You gonna get me killed." Jean understood better than Erie the culture of the Delta in the 1960s.

Betty loved life at Rainbow, but the injustices of both the plantation system and segregated society as a whole became increasingly apparent and a growing concern to both of the Pearsons. As Betty recalled, "When our daughter Erie started school, she went to a two-story brick school in the nearby town of Sumner, while the children of our workers were crowded into a one-room 'school' in the black Baptist church on the farm [plantation]. Every element of society was segregated—schools, restaurants, public restrooms, doctors' offices, even water fountains. We soon learned we were in the very small minority of the white population who believed segregation should end and this country should become a truly open, equal, and free society."

# The Sixties

*The human heart in conflict with itself . . .*
—William Faulkner

*Betty has a manner of expressing herself with humor that is not offensive, not pushing anyone to change, but clear about how she felt.*
—Curtis Wilkie

After the Emmett Till trial, Betty felt as if she was living along the fault line of an earthquake. Two of her most cherished values clashed within her mind and heart. Her family, who believed in the traditional separation of the races, had always been the bedrock of her existence, but equal rights and opportunity for all people constituted her most basic belief. Plus, her personal dilemma was being played out against a background she had never known before: white violence and hatred against blacks. Betty abhorred confrontations, yet she had to stand up for what she believed was right. As racial tensions exploded around the country, her estrangement from her family increased.

At small dinner parties, on the steps of the Sumner Episcopal chapel after Sunday service, or in the clubhouse after a game of golf, Betty and Bill were drawn into talks about politics. She admired Adlai Stevenson: "I really wanted him to win when he ran against Eisenhower for President [in 1952 and 1956]." Betty's most grievous concern, racial segregation, was closer to home. What to do about the stark inequities between the black and white school systems, the deplorable living conditions of the tenant farmers, and the unmitigated racism pervading every inch of Delta culture?

Betty inhaled national news, wanting to know as much as she could about the blacks' dangerous, uphill battle against the racism entrenched throughout the entire nation, but magnified in the South by legalized segregation. She was moved by the stories of brave, resilient black people who courageously demonstrated their sense of purpose. Betty had been deeply impressed with Mamie Till Bradley's dignified composure at the trial and acquittal of the two men who murdered her son. Even more impressive was Till's mother's ability to channel her rage at the injustice of a racist nation, insisting that the casket of her murdered son be left open for his funeral and burial. Mamie Till Bradley wanted to show the world the abominable horror of racism.

At least forty thousand mourners filed through the Chicago funeral home to witness the brutally battered body of Emmett Till, a fourteen-year-old boy beaten beyond recognition and murdered—a black boy accused of making an inappropriate remark to a white woman. Millions more around the world viewed photographs of the atrocity in newspapers and magazines. Betty agreed that Till's mother's outrage lit a spark that ignited the civil rights movement in America. Blacks could no longer tolerate such injustice and abuse. They felt compelled to organize and demonstrate the legitimacy of their cause, to show the nation that all citizens, black and white, are entitled to equal rights, justice, and protection.

In December 1955, in Montgomery, Alabama, three months after the Till trial, Rosa Parks, inspired by Mamie Till Bradley's moral strength, refused to relinquish her seat to a white passenger and move to the back of the bus when instructed to do so by the bus driver. Rosa Parks was arrested. A Montgomery ordinance mandated that public transportation be segregated. Rosa Parks' arrest galvanized the black population of that city to boycott the bus line. Their boycott lasted nearly a year, until the law was changed and segregation on Montgomery buses was abolished. An elderly black woman who took part in the boycott and walked to work every day during that year, said, "My feet are tired, but my soul is at rest because I am walking for the benefit of the next black generation" (David L. Jordan).

As the civil rights movement grew stronger, opposition, particularly in the South, grew increasingly pronounced. Black workers in many local businesses felt trapped. They could be fired on the spot if they gave any indication that they might become active or even supported the movement. More and more, Betty felt she was a stranger in her own country. She felt an ever-growing commitment to black peoples' plight and remembered her grandmother's words, "Betty, God reached down and plucked you from in front of that train because he has something very special he wants you to do with your life." She was compelled to find ways to show her support. Rainbow provided some answers. She and Bill kept in contact with the out-of-town journalists they met during the Till trial. Their home at Rainbow, isolated out in the country, became a refuge, removed from "prying eyes," for visiting reporters, a gathering place for like-minded persons in the Delta—and later, a safe haven for civil rights activists from the north.

In 1959, bishops of the Catholic, Episcopal, and Methodist churches formed the Mississippi Council on Human Relations. Florence Mars and Betty were asked to be board members. Florence, Betty's friend from college and maid of honor at her wedding, was one of the few whites in Neshoba County, Mississippi, who supported civil rights and helped register black voters. Several years later, in the summer of 1964, Florence would cooperate with the FBI in their investigation of the murder of three activists, Michael Schwerner, James Chaney, and Andrew Goodman. She later wrote *Witness in Philadelphia: A Mississippi WASP'S Account of Civil Rights Murders*, which told of her civil rights activities and subsequent ostracism in her hometown.

The purpose of the Human Relations Council, an integrated group, was to further communication between the races and establish a leadership forum to hear about and deal with problems as they arose. Those who organized the council believed meeting and talking to one another was the first step towards building understanding between blacks and whites. It was at these meetings that Betty came to know and admire the courage of black leaders like Aaron Henry, Fannie Lou Hamer, and Amzie Moore. She and Florence were finally meeting other Mississippians who felt as they did. Betty said, "It was good to know there were other white people, scattered across the state, who would join me in fighting for an integrated society."

Having met Aaron Henry at Human Relations Council meetings, Betty drove to Clarksdale to talk with him. Subsequently, she became a card-carrying member of the NAACP: "I had realized by then that my role in the civil rights movement would be largely symbolic—showing that there were white people whose families had been here for generations, but who were ardently opposed to a segregated society. I would actively and openly support the people on the front lines, both Mississippians and civil rights workers, who came into the state, the 'outsiders,' who were being blamed for all of our racial problems."

Although doing so was difficult, Betty learned to accept the growing estrangement from many old friends and townspeople her activities created. But the heightened stress within her family deeply troubled her. She knew what her mother and father believed, and in order to avoid unpleasantness during their frequent visits, she and Bill never talked about race: "Mother was very emotional. She took it personally. She couldn't stand that her circle of friends in Clarksdale thought that Bill and I were 'radical, left-wing nuts.' Mother was embarrassed. She felt betrayed. I always tried to make it easier for them [her parents] if I could. I felt I had to. It was not a pleasant, easy time at all." Years later Betty said, "It is hard to think of good memories during that time, there was so much tension within my family."

There was also mounting tension in the community, and the Pearsons' social world began to close down around them. There were a few—very few—other whites in the area who supported and sympathized with the blacks' struggle for civil rights. Friends began to sort each other out. In small intimate gatherings, Betty and Bill saw more and more of the small cadre of folks who agreed with them. They saw less and less of those who abhorred their involvements. Yet, because of their established social standing and truly good natures, Bill and Betty were still invited to most of the large social functions in the Delta. Simpson/Pearson and Bobo were well established, socially honored, names in the Delta and not to be ostracized. Occasionally, Betty heard of a large gathering to which they were not invited and complained to Bill. He would ask. "Well, do you want to go?" "No, but I'd like to be asked," was always her response.

Through her participation on the advisory committee, Betty met many of the young lawyers and students who were in Mississippi doing civil rights work. John "Jack" Doyle was a young New York lawyer, who had taken a leave of absence from his firm to work with what was called the "President's Committee." He had been sent to Mississippi by the American Bar Association at the request of President Lyndon Johnson. Doyle was a very proper, well-mannered young man, always dressed in coat and tie. His wife, Mary Ellen, was an artist. When Betty learned the couple wasn't going home for Christmas, she invited the Doyles to spend Christmas with them: "Our Christmas tradition in those years was a big family dinner at my parents' home on Christmas Eve and Christmas day dinner at Rainbow with both my parents and Bill's. Everything went well, and I thought that, at least, we had shown them that civil rights workers could be nice people, but that was not to be." Nothing was said at the time, but evidently feelings smoldered:

> Ole Miss played a football game in Jackson the following fall, and we invited Mary Ellen and Jack to go with us, not so much for the game as for the tailgate picnic, which we thought they would enjoy. My father was a rabid Ole Miss fan; for the games in Jackson he had a suite at a local motel and a big spread of food and drinks after each game. After the game we went there, chatted, introduced Mary Ellen and Jack to the other guests, and left thinking everything was fine. Three days later I received a letter (typed by his secretary) from my father informing me Bill and I were always welcome, but he didn't want any more civil rights workers brought to his home or to any party he was giving. I was stunned and hurt and furious that he couldn't even talk to me about it, but had to send an impersonal letter. Needless to say, that was the last time we went to any of their parties. (*Pieces from the Past*, p. 31)

In spite of the growing estrangements, Betty—an upbeat, naturally exuberant woman who liked being with people—worked hard to maintain balance in her life, finding fun in physical activity and creative projects. Participation in a challenging sport was essential for her. She and Bill enjoyed playing golf regularly at the Clarksdale Country Club (Betty's father gave them a membership soon after their marriage, while they dealt with Rainbow's debt). Betty also delighted in an opportunity to play tennis again. Frank Mitchener, a younger friend in Sumner, organized a group of eight or ten families that built a tennis court on a vacant lot in town next to the Episcopal Church.

Betty was a frustrated would-be architect, and her home at Rainbow was a perfect house for her, "because it wasn't fine." She could knock out a wall and start adding on, whenever the notion struck and the money allowed. Always wanting the very best, she assiduously researched to discover what she deemed to be best in design before stating on a project. With her drawing table and the tools to draw her plan to scale, Betty transformed Rainbow without an architect, supervising local carpenters herself.

In 1948, the year after she and Bill moved to Rainbow, they extended the kitchen and changed the back door. The next year, two bathrooms where created where one had been. One had a tub one for the baby and Betty; the other had a shower for Bill. In 1954, a sun porch was added outside the living and dining rooms. The windows (replaceable by screens in the summer) were salvaged from the remodeling of Betty's cousin's house in Clarksdale. Major improvements came in 1959. The Pearsons moved into Sumner for three months, and the whole house was put under one roof. The front door was relocated. A small office (paneled with curly maple from the plantation manager's house) was added. The wall between the living room and the dining room was moved. Fireplaces and floor furnaces were taken out, and central heat and air conditioning were installed. Nine years later, they added a guest suite, using old cypress from demolished (and rebuilt) tenant houses. In 1970, they enlarged Bill's bathroom, and added an exercise room and deck. A wine cellar was built in the mid-'70s, and in 1983 they again enlarged the kitchen. "It was a wonderful kitchen," Betty recalled. There was a long marble counter for rolling out dough and pastry, and the decorative painted tiles with cotton motifs on the cabinets were designed by Leonard Brooks and made in Mexico.

"Gardening and landscape design were my loves, and I spent a lot of time—and Bill would say money—in my gardens." Betty's gardens were an absorbing challenge, one that gave balance to her life and an escape from the mounting personal stress she felt in the early 1960s. When the Pearsons moved to Rainbow, no thought had been given to any type of landscaping. Directly behind the house, their vegetable garden was a large plot of ground plowed by a mule—a rather primitive and not very attractive arrangement. For the first couple of years, Betty hit the books to learn landscape design and gardening from the masters. As Bill gained expertise in growing cotton, Betty absorbed the nuances of landscape design and gardening.

Betty was heavily influenced by Thomas Church, the well-known California landscape architect, who believed a residence and its gardens should be seen as an integrated whole, with out-of-door living spaces treated as separate "rooms" in the overall design. Betty liked the concept and created her own plan. Her design transformed Rainbow into a beautiful—nearly magical—place. She moved the vegetable garden

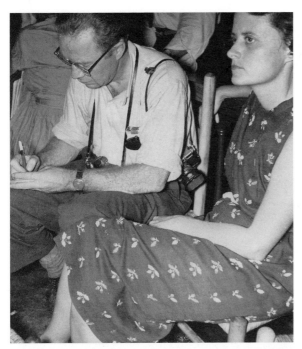

Betty Pearson next to *Life* magazine photographer Ed Clark at Emmett Till trial (1955).

The Emmett Till trial (1955), with the jury seated in the first two rows. At the press table behind the jury are Betty Pearson (caught wiping her brow because of heat) and Florence Mars, the only women allowed behind the bar, other than the court stenographer.

Fincher G. Bobo, Betty's grandfather (on right), and Robert E. Bobo, Betty's father, circa 1920.

Elizabeth "Bessie" Brock Bobo ("Big Mama"), Betty's future grandmother, circa 1898.

Betty's grandmother, Big Mama, circa 1950.

Betty and Bob Bobo growing up at Bobo, mid-1920s.

The commissary at Rainbow, built as a company store in 1914. After mechanization it was changed into a workshop for farm equipment.

Lenora Corley Bobo, Betty's mother, July 1953.

Lt. Erie Elizabeth Bobo, Marine Corps Women's Reserve, World War II.

1st Lt. William Wallace Pearson, US Army Air Corps, World War II.

Betty and Bill's wedding, February 12, 1947. Back row, left to right: George McFall, Hunter Dogan, Patricia Pearson, Mary Martha Presley, Bill Simpson (Bill's uncle), Harvey Henderson (best man), W. L. Robinson (Methodist minister), Bill and Betty Pearson, Robert E. Bobo (Betty's father), Florence Mars (maid of honor), Guy Clark, Gee Wright, Bob Bobo (Betty's brother). Front row, left to right: Sonny Simpson (Bill's cousin), Emily Jean Corley (flower girl and Betty's first cousin), Kathryn Keeler (Betty's cousin), Georgie Haaga, Ray Mabry (Bill's cousin).

Betty Bobo Pearson in the 1970s.

Lining up for the march to commemorate Dr. Martin Luther King Jr. on the anniversary of his assassination. Memphis, April 1969. Right to left: Jean Fisher, Brad Foster, Carl Walters, Betty Pearson.

Betty Pearson in march.

Others in march.

Crowd gathered to hear Ted Kennedy speak and Peter, Paul and Mary sing at conclusion of march.

Erie Pearson and Jean
Tucker, July 1957.

A section of Betty's
garden, August 1965.

The swimming pool at Rainbow, August 1984.

Bi-weekly swimming class at Rainbow, summer 1986. Every child at Rainbow, except one, learned to swim.

Walter and Puddin Tucker at their daughter Nanny's wedding, June 12, 1982.

Women featured in the award-winning film *Standing on My Sisters' Shoulders*, Tougaloo College, April 2003. Left to right: Victoria Gray Adams, Joan Mulholland, Constance Slaughter-Harvey, Betty Bobo Pearson, Flonzie Brown-Wright, Dorrie Ladner, Gloria Dickerson, June Elizabeth Johnson.

Bill Pearson receives the *Cotton Grower* achievement award in 1983.

Betty and Bill at home.

Betty accepting the annual award given an older adult of distinction, presented by Leading Age California, May 2015.

further back on their property, and placed and planted a[t]
tractive, eye-appealing garden areas around the house. Sh[e]
put in a brick walk leading to an acre of vegetables that gr[e]w
in a series of huge raised beds. These large raised plots w[e]
at first bordered with railroad crossties. These wooden b[or]
ders were later replaced with low brick retaining walls, [w]
brick paths leading between the beds. Betty rearranged [her]
gardens and their paths the way other people rearrang[e] [fur]
niture inside their houses.

As Betty implemented her landscape design, she w[as]
a full view of her handiwork from inside the house[.]
Betty's brother, spoke of the time he was visiting his[,]
four or five years after the Pearsons moved to Rainbo[w]
were having lunch [in her dining room], and she sai[d to the]
man who worked for her, 'Walter get the saw.' Betty [had the]
saw and cut right through the wall beneath the wind[ow. She]
wanted a door leading to her gardens, making th[e dining]
room open and inviting. When Betty envisioned [a]
larger room, or a better arrangement of walls, sh[e was her]
own architect and construction supervisor.

The house and garden were an extension of B[etty]
and sense of style. Her excellent taste, the hos[pitality she]
created, reflects her personality. She surround[ed]
Rainbow with a huge, magnanimous welcome. [Everyone felt]
home, at ease. She was never frou-frou or pre[tentious. She]
was always comfortable but correct. She made [Rainbow]
the very best home she could imagine.

In the gardens, as big as a truck farm, Bett[y said,]
"We had everything you can grow in Mississ[ippi and some]
things you can't. There were beds of aspar[agus, rad]
ish, strawberries, raspberries, parsley and ev[ery herb]
imaginable. Then every spring we planted [to]
matoes (forty or fifty plants), onions of se[veral]

low squash and zucchini, string beans, butter beans, peas, potatoes, bell peppers, and around eight or ten different hot peppers, and anything that looked interesting in the seed catalogs I poured over every January." One of her specialties was the baby vegetables, fully ripe miniature vegetables cultivated for perfection and a more tender, delicate taste. In addition, Betty said,

> I planted cutting flowers in the vegetable garden—zinnias and marigolds mainly, and had other flowers like daylilies and other lilies, and daisies, and flowers I can't remember, scattered around the house in various places in with the shrubs . . . hostas and ferns under the trees and daffodils, including some from my grandmother's garden, everywhere. There were a couple of big oak trees Bill's aunt had planted, plus peach and pear trees, and pecan trees in the pasture. I added hawthorns, Japanese maples and other small trees and, eventually, a greenhouse where we started our own seeds.

While Bill's ongoing experimentation for improving methods of growing cotton earned Rainbow the reputation as a research farm, Betty was conducting her own research. She ordered dozens of small perennials every spring in order to discover which plants did well in the Delta and those that did not. She tried artichokes for a couple of years, and although they grew well and looked good, they were bitter. Jerusalem artichokes, however, did fine.

Puddin was Betty's right hand in the garden and loved working in the greenhouse. Under Betty's direction, she managed much of the activity. Although Rosie was the cook, Puddin also had her specialties in the kitchen: biscuits—sometimes three hundred at a time—and Jerusalem

artichoke pickles. Disdaining the way most folks used the food processor to make their pickles, Puddin said, "I tell you the truth, that ain't no way to make a relish, without peeling and chopping the artichokes by hand—scrubbin's not good enough. Unless you have it right you don't have it. Miss Betty and I got along fine. Sometimes there'd be little fusses, but never a lasting grudge. They were having company all the time. They'd usually be gone in January and February and left me and Walter with the keys. We'd have to take care of visitors then. When she got back, she'd tell me to go home and rest."

Carolyn Webb often visited and "played" at Rainbow before the Pearsons moved to town and became the Webbs' next-door neighbors in Sumner. Carolyn recalled, "Betty's elaborate maze of raised beds looked complicated, huge. You name it, she grew it. She had six different types of peppers. Her garden stretched around a big, old house, very elegant inside. Betty had plenty of help, lots of folks who worked for them, took care of them, who were always coming in and out, [easy and relaxed]. Rainbow, Betty's little piece of paradise was just the way Betty's heart is—always welcoming."

The Pearsons kept horses for Erie, and after the grandchildren arrived, Betty finally talked Bill into building a swimming pool, a beauty in its own garden behind a pool house. Also for the grandchildren, they built a huge square brick bed filled with sand in a corner of the vegetable garden under a pecan tree. Betty was still designing new areas of the garden when they sold the land and moved to Sumner in 1991. Betty said, "It was the main reason for my deep sadness over leaving. It was beautiful."

In the summer of 1961, SNCC (the Student Nonviolent Coordinating Committee), founded earlier that spring, joined forces with another civil rights group, CORE (Congress of Racial Equality). Over a thousand "Freedom Riders," black and white student volunteers, took bus trips in racially mixed groups through the South to test the new laws prohibiting segregation in interstate bus and railway stations. The Freedom Riders brought national attention to the states' disregard for federal law and the lack of police protection from uncontrolled violence. As the Freedom Riders traveled through Mississippi and other southern states, the local police arrested and jailed them on charges of trespassing, unlawful assembly, and violation of local ordinances. In some places, the local police, cooperating with the Ku Klux Klan, stepped aside and allowed mobs to attack the students.

Lomax Lamb from Marks, Mississippi, who was a good friend of the Pearsons and a frequent visitor at Rainbow, shared their interest in and support of civil rights. Lamb, a graduate of Yale Law School, kept up with many of his Yankee friends, some of whom contacted him the summer of 1962, asking him to "look after our kids" as they headed south. That summer, and in the turbulent summers that followed, Betty offered the student volunteers from the north safe haven at Rainbow whenever they wanted to take a break during their ride through the state.

Throughout the summer the newspapers carried articles about James Meredith, an African American Air Force veteran with sixty hours of transferrable credits, who applied for admission to the University of Mississippi in the spring of 1961. When his application was rejected, he filed suit in the US District Court for the Southern District of Mississippi, alleging his rejection was based on race. After twenty-one months of legal wrangling, his case reached the US Supreme Court, which ordered the university to admit Meredith immediately. In spite of Mississippi Governor Ross Barnett's all-out efforts to block Meredith's enrollment, on September 13, the district court entered an injunction directing members of the board of trustees and officials of the University of Mississippi to register Meredith—even though the state legislature's had passed emergency measures to prevent this eventuality. With the backing of the courts, on September 20 Meredith tried again to gain admission. He was rebuffed by university officials. Angry crowds demonstrating against Meredith's admission began to gather in Oxford. Alarmed that the demonstrations would turn violent, President John Kennedy telephoned the governor daily to urge voluntary compliance with the court order; he did not want to send in federal troops. The governor insisted he needed more time. Attorney General Robert Kennedy, monitoring the growing unrest, maintained constant contact with the Department of Justice officials serving in Mississippi. In an effort to avoid potential violence, President Kennedy threatened to arrest Governor Barnett if Meredith was not admitted by the first of October.

On Saturday, September 29, Betty and Bill drove to Jackson to watch the Ole Miss Rebels play football against the Kentucky Wildcats. Although the stadium was filled with waving Confederate flags, they were shocked when a gigantic Confederate flag was unveiled on the field at halftime, and the crowd shouted, "We want Ross!" Governor Barnett appeared on the field amidst the marching bands, grabbed the microphone, and declared, "I love Mississippi! I love her people! I love and I respect our heritage." When he said he would never allow a colored person into the University of Mississippi because he respected Mississippi's heritage, the crowd exploded with ear-splitting cheers. Everyone stood, waving their flags—everyone except Betty and Bill Pearson, who looked at each other in horror and remained seated. Bill turned to Betty and said, "We may be killed if we don't stand up." She responded, "I'm not moving."

The next afternoon, over three thousand individuals—students, locals, and Klan groups from Florida to Texas—encouraged by the governor's stand, assembled in Oxford to protest the university's decision to obey the law. Meredith was to be admitted the next morning. Two thousand US marshals were unable to quell the riot that ensued. Two people were killed and sixty marshals injured amidst a hail of bricks, sticks, bottles, and homemade bombs. President Kennedy then sent five thousands federal troops to Oxford to quell the violence, and James Meredith became the first Negro to become a student at the University of Mississippi.

Norbert Schlei, another of Lomax Land's friends from student days at Yale, was Robert Kennedy's assistant in charge of the Office of General Counsel. Schlei was sent to Oxford that weekend to oversee the situation, and joined Chief Marshal James McShane and Assistant Attorney General for Civil Rights John Doar in advising the president to send in troops. After relative calm returned to Oxford, Land invited Schlei out to Rainbow for a few days of relaxation. Schlei stayed only one night; he was called back to Washington to advise President Kennedy on the handling of the Cuban Missile Crisis.

A year after the riots, Land brought the author Walter Lord, who had been his roommate at Yale, for a brief visit at Rainbow. Lord, an established author from New York City best known for his documentary-style nonfiction, wanted to get a taste of the Delta and plantation life. Gathering material and interviewing people for his book *The Past That Would Not Die* (1965), he wanted to understand Mississippi's violent resistance to integration. While at Rainbow, Lord mentioned he wanted to meet William Winter. Betty said she'd call Winter. Lord, shaking his head, said, "I've never seen anything like your society in Mississippi. You folks just pass someone from one person to another, hand to hand, all over Mississippi." •

Betty described how this Northerner came to breakfast impeccably dressed on the morning Oscar Carr and Land were taking Lord to Calhoun County to meet some "red-neck-hill-people," who trained Oscar's dogs. Betty then noticed that Lord had put his cashmere sweater on inside out. He nodded, "Well I thought I should look a little seedy." Betty could only shake her head and laugh, doubting that Walter Lord could ever look seedy. The interview later that day not only gave the author insight into a different culture, it proved a brutal eye-opener for Carr, who dealt with these folks regularly. One of the men who trained his dogs said, "A nigger is just like a chicken or a duck, it hasn't got a soul."

By 1963, civil rights battles were raging across the nation. Betty, more deeply involved at the local level, attended a human relations conference at Tougaloo College. There she heard the report of the Mississippi Advisory Committee to the United States Civil Rights Commission. Over a fourteen-month period ending in January 1963, the committee had organized a total of six open hearings in Jackson, Greenville, Clarksdale, and Meridian. They received approximately 150 complaints of "alleged denial of equal protection of the law." The report submitted to the Civil Rights Commission stated,

> The [Mississippi Advisory] Committee regrets that its
> fact-finding efforts were actively opposed by agents and in-
> strumentalities of the State Government. . . . Investigations
> have indicated that in all important areas of citizenship, a
> Negro in Mississippi receives substantially less than his due
> consideration as an American and as a Mississippian. This

denial extends from the time he is denied the right to be born in a non-segregated hospital, through his segregated and inferior school years and his productive years when jobs for which he can qualify are refused, to the day he dies and is laid to rest in a cemetery for Negroes only.

Although the Committee received a large number of sworn complaints from citizens denied the right to vote, the report focused on one particular area: police brutality. Seven complaints related to the maltreatment of Negroes were included in the report: brutal beatings; forceful evictions at gunpoint; arrests with no evidence; confinements in "the hot box" (an unventilated jail cell) for days with no food; exorbitant fines; and police (though present) offering no protection to Negroes attacked by mobs of whites (Report of Mississippi by the Mississippi Advisory Committee to the United States Commission on Civil Rights). A later report of the Civil Rights Commission stated that local officials failed to enforce the law. From January 1961 to May 1964, more than 150 serious incidents of racial violence were reported in Mississippi: thirty-five shootings, thirty bombings, thirty-five church burnings, eighty beatings, and at least six murders. In only a few cases were those responsible arrested or prosecuted.

When Betty was asked to join the Mississippi Advisory Committee to the United States Civil Rights Commission, created in 1959, she said yes. Few white Mississippians were willing to serve on this biracial committee. A few days after her appointment, an article appeared in the *Memphis Commercial Appeal* announcing the names of the members of the committee. That morning Betty's father arrived at the Pearsons' door, newspaper in hand and "literally in tears." He begged Betty not to serve on the integrated committee, telling her, "It would make you a traitor to your people and your heritage." Betty loved her parents—especially her father—and she did not want to hurt him, but in this case she saw no choice:

> If I was to live with myself for the rest of my life, I had to be
> true to what I knew was right. I said, "But Dad, all my life
> you've taught me to do what I know is right, regardless of
> the consequences or the opinions of others." I think that it
> had never occurred to him that my idea of what was right
> would ever be different from his. Thus began what was
> the most painful period of my life. I do not compare my
> experience with that of the true heroines of the civil rights
> movement, those brave black women who were arrested
> and beaten time after time, only to come back and try once
> more to register to vote.

Many times, late in the night when Betty answered the phone, an unidentified caller made threats to her property and person, but she claimed, "That's all they were—only threats." She may have never felt she was in physical danger, but Puddin took no chances. She said, "Whenever I drove with Miss Betty, Walter would say, 'Don't forget your gun.' Some people just didn't like seeing white and black folks riding in a car together, both on the front seat." Although Betty said she never felt any physical danger, the emotional stress resulting from her parents' unhappiness and the disapproval of many of her old friends was hurtful and constant. She tried to maintain a quasi-normal relationship with her parents "for the sake of Erie, our daughter, their first grandchild, whom they adored. It wasn't easy at best, and sometimes very painful. It was never more than an armed truce."

But pain, mental or physical, never stopped Betty. In 1965,

in addition to emotional turmoil, she experienced severe internal pain. Her doctor recommended a cystocele and rectocele repair. What was to be a relatively simple surgical procedure led to complications, and she was unable to urinate naturally after the operation: "I was in the hospital in Clarksdale for at least two weeks, and recovered enough that I left the hospital every morning with a catheter inserted and closed with a clip, drove myself home to Rainbow and stayed all day, drove myself back to hospital late in the afternoon, had a nurse remove the catheter and tried all night to urinate naturally." This was Betty's routine until she took Valium, which helped her to "relax," for a short time. Then her "plumbing" began to function properly, and she resumed all activities with full force.

The Mississippi Advisory Committee to the United States Civil Rights Commission held monthly meetings in Jackson, and reported to the national commission once a year. In the mid-1960s, before the national committee's annual meeting in Washington, DC, the attorney for the local school board called Betty and asked her to talk with someone in Washington "who could give her information that would be helpful to the school board." In 1954, the US Supreme Court had ruled that segregated schools were unconstitutional, and that such schools should be integrated with all deliberate speed.

Betty "took the assignment seriously," and while in Washington—in addition to attending the commission meeting—she sought out and talked with officials in the Department of Justice about how to achieve school integration in the best possible way. The people she met with assured her they understood Mississippi's problems in integrating their schools, and said they would work with local officials to move slowly. Betty remembered, "When I got home I called the attorney and told him I had what I felt was good news. The people to whom I had talked understood the problems involved in integrating schools in a county like ours, where there was a large majority of black students and where the public schools had been so unequal. What they wanted was 'intent' to integrate and if we came up with a reasonable plan, they would give us the years we would need to implement it. I suggested that we could integrate the first grade each year, and in twelve years the schools would be integrated." Betty was stunned when the attorney said he was not even going to tell the school board what she reported. He had hoped Betty could tell them some way to avoid the process: "We will never integrate our schools." "In that case," Betty warned, "instead of doing it gradually, and on your own terms, the schools would be integrated suddenly, by court order." Which is exactly what happened.

In these years, Oscar and Billie Carr from Clarksdale were frequent guests at Betty and Bill's small dinner parties. When Bob Bobo, Betty's younger brother, skipped kindergarten and was promoted to first grade, he met Oscar Carr, another first grader. The two five-year-old boys became best friends, riding horses and bikes, attending Boy Scout meetings and camp, playing high school sports, double dating—always together until high school graduation, when Oscar went off to Annapolis, and Bob headed to Ole Miss. Over the years they were growing up, Oscar spent so much time at the Bobo house, Betty said, "I had two younger brothers, Oscar and Bob."

Oscar matured into a tall, handsome young man with a charismatic personality. When Betty was in the Marine Corps during World War II, Oscar, an Annapolis graduate and naval officer, was on a ship docked in Long Beach for a few days before heading to the Pacific. He called Betty, who was stationed close-by at El Toro, and asked to visit her. As Betty drove him back to his ship, they stopped at a traffic signal, where two young, attractive girls stood chatting. Oscar opened his door, stepped out of the car, and said, "Watch this." Betty remembered saying, "Oh, Oscar quit showing off." While she watched and waited, Oscar and the two girls disappeared into a bar. Betty declared, "He was probably the best-looking thing they'd seen in a long time." The three appeared about thirty minutes later, laughing like old friends. Oscar took great delight in showing "his big sister" how easily he could turn a lady's head.

After they were both married (Oscar married Billie Fisher from Memphis) and once again living in the Delta, the Pearsons and the Carrs saw a great deal of each other. Betty said, "Oscar and Billie were a great deal more conservative than we were." When she talked about her civil rights activities, Oscar listened, but did not say much. He was busy establishing himself at Mascot, the Carr plantation, and in Clarksdale he was instrumental in the establishment of the First National Bank of Clarksdale and the first chairman of its board. Betty recalled that it was about five years after the Till trial when Oscar told her the most "amazing" story. He said, "I was driving home from Memphis, and when I came down that last hill into the Delta, all of a sudden I saw one of those tenant houses for the first time." Oscar continued, "Although I had seen such houses all of my life on Mascot and other plantations, I never before thought about people living in that shack with no electricity, no plumbing. . . ." Betty said, "It was like a thunderbolt out of the blue. . . . One of those 'road to Damascus' things where you have a sudden conversion."

Oscar Carr "jumped in with both feet, with incredible enthusiasm and energy to help improve the economic conditions of the blacks in our area. Oscar and I became bosom buddies." Economic and educational development grants to help black people were available through President Lyndon Johnson's "Great Society." Oscar and his brother, Andy Carr, worked hard to bring federal money to Coahoma County. Andy became president of Coahoma Opportunities Inc., an anti-poverty action group that distributed over $2 million a year for programs like legal aide, neighborhood centers, and Head Start. Andy said Oscar was outspoken, involved in politics, and active in his support of black candidates. He campaigned for Charles Evers, the older brother of slain civil rights activist Medgar Evers, in his race for mayor of Fayette, Mississippi. In 1969, Charles Evers became the first black man to be elected mayor of a Mississippi town since the Reconstruction era. Hodding Carter III, who became assistant secretary of state in Jimmy Carter's administration, said, "It would have been very comfortable for him [Oscar] to be just a cocktail party liberal. Instead he got committed and involved."

However, Oscar's unrestrained, active involvement in the civil rights cause offended some of the more conservative board members of the First National Bank of Clarksdale, which he had helped to establish. By 1971, concerned with the "image" Oscar's political activities created, those conservative members organized a secret ballot to oust him as chairman and eliminate him from the board. The vote was taken, and Oscar lost. Andy, his brother and a member of the board, was outraged: "Without Oscar there wouldn't be a bank." Although the ballot was secret, Andy determined he would find out how the fifteen members had voted. He discovered that six members voted to retain Oscar, with nine voting to oust him. Bob Bobo was one of the nine. That day

Andy not only resigned from the board, "I resigned from the bank." Andy moved his accounts.

Betty, "shocked beyond words," could not comprehend how her brother could betray his best friend, but Betty never said a word to Bob about his vote. She believes actions speak louder than words, and Bob had "spoken." His opposition to integration was stronger than his loyalty to Oscar. She and her brother were diametrically opposed on the question of integration, but both worked to maintain an aura of civility at family gatherings. Not wanting to become further estranged from her family, she knew confronting Bob would drive a deeper wedge—or possibly sever their already severely strained relationship. Betty, who continued to feel bonded with her father, asked him about Bob's treatment of Oscar. She knew he agreed with Bob on racial issues, but loyalty to friends and family was a driving force in his life. Betty's was an unanswerable question for a man whose family, his world, was being torn apart. He responded, "I'll never understand."

# Tumultuous Times

*The 1960s . . . the dams of tradition burst.*
—Daniel Henninger

*We would like to live as we once lived, but history will not permit it.*
—John F. Kennedy

The 1960s was a turbulent decade on many fronts across the nation: traditions were abandoned; security was threatened; civil rights were demanded; demonstrations turned violent; campuses saw protest; bras were publicly burned; hippies decamped to communes; young people practiced free love; and the threat of communism, feared by some as subversion from within, was feared as an outside missiles threat. Civil rights activist Medgar Evers was assassinated on June 12, 1963. President John F. Kennedy was assassinated on November 22, 1963. Civil rights activist Malcolm X was assassinated on February 21, 1965. Dr. Martin Luther King, leader of the civil rights movement, was assassinated on April 4, 1968. Robert Kennedy, presidential candidate and former attorney general, was assassinated on June 6, 1968. The nation witnessed a massive shift in behavior, as the passionate tearing down of established ways was met with equally fervent resistance to change.

By 1960 Betty was serving on the Mississippi Council on Human Relations and supporting the civil rights activities in her state. The leaders of SNCC told her they were finding intense and often violent resistance by segregationists in the rural areas of Mississippi. Direct action campaigns, which were successful in urban areas of the South such as Montgomery and Birmingham, were not possible in Mississippi. In order to prove to the federal government and the nation that black Mississippians wanted to vote and would vote if not impeded by terror and intimidation, SNCC organized a "Freedom Vote" in the summer of 1963. In mock elections held throughout Mississippi, some eighty thousand blacks symbolically voted for Aaron Henry, a local activist running for governor, and Ed King, a white chaplain from Tougaloo College who acted as Henry's running mate. Betty was impressed with the success of the Freedom Vote and felt encouraged.

In 1964, COFO (the Council of Federated Organizations) coordinated the efforts of all civil rights groups for a summer-long protest in Mississippi, to be called the "Freedom Summer." White student volunteers from the North were recruited to join with local black Mississippians to help accomplish three ambitious goals: 1) the registration of as many black voters as possible; 2) the establishment of "Freedom Schools" for literacy and political instruction; 3) the creation of a local leadership network. Betty would play a substantial role in the local network. Others in the movement recognized her as a natural leader with well-honed organizational skills. She had a habit of authority, but she was fair-minded and supportive of others' individuality. Co-workers respected her and followed what she said. People trusted her upbeat, sometimes plucky, straightforward honesty. Reynolds Cheney, an Episcopal priest in the Delta at the time, spoke of Betty's strong sense of social justice. She was determined to express her opinion, but with "a unique spirit that made you feel good. You felt better from talking to her."

Betty's bond with black leaders like Aaron Henry, Fannie Lou Hamer, and Amzie Moore strengthened, and her relationship with white friends with whom she shared the same values deepened. However, as Mississippi became the national battleground for civil rights, Betty's estrangement from her family and most of her friends calcified—with one important exception. Bill Pearson, Betty's husband, was her bedrock of support. In those years Bill, responsible for managing and improving Rainbow, was not as actively involved in the movement as Betty, but he encouraged her and stood firmly behind her activities. These two shared the conviction that segregation must end. Rainbow Plantation, isolated out in the country, and removed from the violent discord occurring in most towns and rural communities throughout Mississippi that summer, was a tranquil oasis away from contention and strife. A place where blacks were respected and liked to work, it was a welcoming stopover for student volunteers from the North and government agents and lawyers involved in civil rights litigation.

It had been a hundred years since the Civil War culturally dislocated and economically devastated Mississippi, which had been the fifth richest state in the nation before that war. A decade after the war, although still wretchedly poor, Mississippians were adjusting to the social, political, and economic upheaval caused by the conflict, the end of slavery, and Reconstruction. Negroes voted, held offices, and owned land and businesses. Apart from the few whites who owned large tracts of land, race and their "sacred" Southern heritage were the only things that distinguished most white Mississippians from their Negro counterparts. The loss of status festered in the hearts of poor white men, who struggled to compete with black men to scratch out a living as tenant farmers or hired hands. By the 1890s, white politicians began enacting Jim Crow laws, trading on the frustrations and fears of their white constituents. These laws disenfranchised blacks and segregated every aspect of life in hospitals, restaurants, hotels, movie theaters, cemeteries—even down to rest rooms and water fountains. Jim Crow laws also effectively blocked Negroes from adequate education.

Although plantation owners were also affected by Mississippi's weak economy, land (usually inherited) still provided position and power. And landed Mississippians typically enjoyed a more genial relationship with Negroes—"as long as they were kept in their place." Most of the landed families practiced a type of noblesse oblige, befriending and taking care of the blacks who worked their property and cared for them personally. These landowners also maintained pleasant relations with those Negroes who lived in their own separate communities and worked independently.

Freedom Summer of 1964 tested this paternalism. Most of those with land, like Betty's father, wanted to preserve the old ways and keep the Negroes in their place, although they did not like or support the violent subversion espoused by the Ku Klux Klan. The violent troublemakers constituted about 10 percent of the total white population of Mississippi. Most Mississippians, wanting only to be left alone, turned their backs on the civil, cultural, and economic inequities, and hoped that the troubles would disappear. Very few whites openly sympathized with and supported the Negroes' plight.

The information Betty gathered and the hatred she witnessed made her heartsick, as she watched the basic civility of earlier years unravel. The summer of 1964 was a violent season. What happened in Philadelphia, Mississippi, where three COFO workers were murdered, was a microcosm of the violence happening throughout the state. Florence Mars, Betty's best friend since college, who served on the Human Relations Council with her, lived in Philadelphia. Florence witnessed firsthand how law and civility broke down when the white citizens in her small, friendly town felt that their Southern way of life was threatened. Betty felt personally involved with her friend's sanity and safety. Florence's experience in Philadelphia echoed the complex challenges Betty experienced as a leader on both the Mississippi Council on Human Relations and the Advisory Committee to the National Civil Rights Commission.

On Sunday, June 21, 1964, during a hot, lazy, after-church afternoon in Philadelphia, Florence picked up a copy of the *New Orleans Times-Picayune* dated Tuesday, June 16, and read, "The night riders struck Neshoba County, when a Negro church [Mt. Zion] was surrounded by armed white men, most of them masked. Three Negroes attending a church board meeting were beaten and chased away. A short time later the church went up in flames." These events had happened five days earlier—and less than ten miles away from the house where Florence lived. Perplexed as to why she had not heard or read a word about this event, Florence went the next day to see the editor of the local newspaper, the *Neshoba Democrat*, to ask why the story had not been reported locally. The editor, Jack Tannehill, a white man, said the story had come off the AP wire service from New York. When he went to check it out, he could find "no reliable witnesses." He spoke with Bud Cole, a black man and church member, who said he was beaten as he was leaving a board meeting at Mt. Zion that evening. The editor said he had doubts about Cole's story and suggested members of the Mt. Zion community had been party to the burning.

Concerned and even more perplexed after her visit with Tannehill, Florence told Betty she knew what the editor told her was impossible. She was familiar with the Mt. Zion church. She knew the people who lived in the area. It was an old, established community of Negro landowners long respected by the white community in Neshoba County. Their church meant much to them. It was the center of life for these people. Plus, she knew Bud Cole. He was a quiet and dignified man. His word was reliable. If he said he was beaten, he had been beaten.

Tannehill had mentioned that the three civil rights workers, who had arrived in town the day before to investigate the church burning, had been reported missing by COFO. He said, "They were speeding out here and got themselves put in jail. Of course they [the police] turned them loose after they [the civil rights workers] paid a fine, and now they [COFO] say they are missing." Florence asked, "Why would COFO say they were missing if they weren't?" The editor said, "They'll do anything to raise money. This is just the kind of hoax they'll pull on us, and then we get all the [bad] publicity for it."

From the television news, Betty and Florence learned that Michael Schwerner (a twenty-four-year-old white, Jewish male from New York City), James Chaney (a twenty-one-year-old black male from Meridian, Mississippi), and Andrew Goodman (a twenty-one-year-old white, Jewish male from New York City) were missing. After talking with people in the Mt. Zion community, the three young men headed out of Neshoba County on a main highway. As they drove through Philadelphia, they were arrested by Deputy Sheriff Cecil Price on a charge of speeding and jailed at about

4:00 in the afternoon. At 10:30 that night, after they paid a twenty-dollar fine, Price released them. He said he told them to see how fast they could get out of the county. He followed them in a police car to the edge of town, and last saw them driving south on Highway 19 toward Meridian. "And then they disappeared."

As the two friends discussed the news, Florence said she knew it was not a hoax and was surprised and worried people in town were saying they "knew that COFO had arranged the disappearance to make us look bad so they can raise money in other parts of the country." When the young men's station-wagon was found abandoned and burned, twelve miles north of Philadelphia, the discovery had no impact on public opinion. Both Betty and Florence saw Deputy Sheriff Price say on TV he watched the boys driving south.

Florence continued to hear comments:

"They had no business down here."
"We don't think anything has happened to them, but if it has, they got what they deserved."
"This wouldn't have happened if they had stayed home where they belonged."
"How long do you think we'd last in Harlem?"

The people of Philadelphia did not want to believe any of their citizens would violate the law or, worse yet, commit murder. The idea of a hoax was strongly reinforced by newspaper articles and leaflets, and a solid wall of resistance was thrown up to prevent the invasion of any outsiders into Neshoba County. The US senator from Mississippi, James Eastland, said at the time, "Mississippians were attempting to preserve the peace in the face of a Communist-backed conspiracy to thrust violence upon them."

A day after the disappearance of the three civil rights volunteers, Karl Fleming of *Newsweek* and Claude Sitton of the *New York Times*, interviewed Sheriff Rainey and Deputy Sheriff Price at the courthouse. As the reporters stepped out of the sheriff's office into the hall, a group of prominent, church-going Philadelphia businessmen surrounded the two and threatened them with violence if they didn't get out of town fast. The reporters crossed the street, entered a store, and asked the shopkeeper behind the counter to intervene on their behalf. The elderly white gentleman listened to their request for help, and in a soft voice said, "If you were a nigger and they were out there in the street beating you to death, I don't expect I'd go out and give them a hand, but they're absolutely right. If the nigger lovers and outside agitators would stay out of here and leave us alone, there wouldn't be any trouble."

Earlier that spring, Florence told Betty that during the night of April 5, twelve crosses were burned in Neshoba County. Sheriff Rainey and the local newspaper editorials blamed outside agitators. Florence knew local people must have been involved: "It would be impossible for strangers to come in and burn the crosses simultaneously without being seen." She sent Betty a copy of one of the circulars distributed to every house in the white community a few weeks later. The Ku Klux Klan was defined as a "Christian, democratic, politically independent, pro-American organization dedicated to total segregation of the races and destruction of Communism. Jews, Turks, Mongels [sic], Tarters [sic], Orientals, Negroes, Papists, or any other person whose native background or culture is foreign to the Anglo-Saxon system of government of responsible FREE individual Citizens" were not acceptable. Printed in bold black letters were twenty reasons for joining the White Knights of the Ku Klux Klan of Mississippi. One of the reasons given was, "It is a secret organization and no one will know you are a member."

On June 23, two days after Goodman, Schwerner, and Chaney were reported missing, President Johnson issued a statement indicating that the federal government would "spare no effort" in finding out what had happened in Neshoba County. The next day, FBI agents—easily recognized because of their white shirts, dark trousers and briefcases—swarmed into town. Within ten days, four hundred US Navy sailors, working in shifts, began dredging the swamps and combing the area for miles around, searching for the bodies of the three civil rights volunteers. The white community felt besieged. People resented the federal intrusion, believing their local law enforcement was "perfectly capable" of handling the case. There was even greater animosity towards the reporters (as was demonstrated towards Fleming and Sitton) arriving from around the world to present "unfair stories blown out of all proportion."

On Friday after the reported disappearance, a farmer who lived close to the Mt. Zion community told his neighbor, who repeated the tale to Florence, that the Ku Klux Klan had murdered the boys. The farmer had said he hated, "what had happened, but some of his relatives were involved, and there wasn't anything he could do about it if he planned to continue living in Neshoba County." Florence said she was not surprised by this revelation, only dismayed that all around her, neighbors were choking out the spirit of inquiry, holding their tongues. No one wanted to talk about the disappearances—or if they did, their words conformed to the communal defensive denial that anyone in Neshoba County could be involved. But Florence's Aunt Ellen, whom Betty had called a "spit-fire," was an independent-minded woman, never afraid to voice her opinions. Aunt Ellen made it plain that she suspected the Klan—and that she felt Sheriff Rainey was a member. Florence also spoke with a few women Catholic friends who said they suspected the Klan. Catholics, having long been a target of the Klan, were familiar with the group's methods.

Betty could hardly wait to tell Bill what Florence's Aunt Ellen had done when she heard Neshoba County residents being interviewed on the radio. The only responses were, "They got what they deserved," and "They had no business down here." Aunt Ellen phoned the station and asked if these were the only answers they were getting. When told that they were, she said, "Well, I am a citizen of Neshoba and I do not feel that way. Furthermore, I'm waiting on the FBI agents, who are supposed to be making a house-to-house canvas." Two hours later, two agents showed up at Aunt Ellen's apartment. Agent Phil Slayden later reported to his fellow agents, "We've finally found someone who will talk to us." Aunt Ellen was the first citizen in Neshoba County to treat the FBI to some "Southern hospitality"—which in her case involved truth telling. The next week, after two agents called on Florence, Aunt Ellen and Florence began to meet regularly with the agents. Although neither Florence nor Aunt Ellen could help find Schwerner, Chaney, and Goodman, they knew the people of the county and the "community character."

Betty admired and praised Florence's actions, but with the situation in Philadelphia becoming increasingly tense, she was worried. In mid-July, she decided to pay Florence a visit. She got in her car and drove the three hours down to Philadelphia. While the two friends wandered around town, Betty noted how respectable business owners—and even Florence's neighbors—were closed-mouthed, edgy, and in denial about the possibility of criminal behavior on the part of anyone in their town. On Sunday, when the friends went to the Methodist church, where Florence taught Sunday School, people avoided talking about the "elephant in the room"—the COFO volunteers' disappearance. Because membership in the Klan was secret, it was impossible to know if the curtain of silence was due to loyalty to the "cause" or fear of recrimination, but it seemed obvious to the two women the Ku Klux Klan was controlling the thoughts of the white citizenry of Neshoba County. Florence herself had been warned by an observant friend that she was under surveillance; the Klan was watching her.

When Betty and Florence went into town that week, they observed a small group of men checking all out-of-county license plates so as to identify and often harass every journalist and outsider who arrived in Philadelphia. They closely watched and recorded every move made by an FBI agent. One local man who struck up a street corner conversation with an agent, said he was later shunned by long-time friends. Florence showed Betty the Steak House Café, the Klan's central meeting place a block off the town square. She said when the Civil Rights Act passed three weeks earlier, on July 2, outlawing racial segregation by facilities that served the general public (known as "public accommodations"), the cafe became a private club with white sheets hung in the windows.

After Betty drove back to Rainbow, she and Florence stayed in near daily contact. They felt certain the Klan members knew murder had been committed in Philadelphia, that the Klan was responsible for the murders, and that membership reached deep into the town's power structure—even into Sheriff Rainey's office. Yet, Florence said almost every white person in the community continued to proclaim, with ardor, that the affair was all a "hoax," and that COFO workers were the perpetrators. COFO evoked a hatred among the whites in Neshoba County that contributed to the community's belligerent response to the press, the FBI, and the federal government. COFO was the "embodiment of evil, of everything white Mississippians found most despicable." Frustrated and disheartened, Florence told Betty, in one of their frequent phone calls, that she was cooperating as much as she could with the FBI investigation. She felt those responsible for murder had to be brought to justice. Betty agreed, but when she hung up the phone, she told Bill, "I'm worried about Flossie."

On Tuesday, August 4, the bodies of Michael Schwerner, James Chaney, and Andrew Goodman were found in a newly constructed earthen dam beneath fifteen feet of dirt. The discovery shattered the "hoax" rationale, but not the anger against the Northern invaders. Some locals claimed the FBI had secretly buried the bodies, and the animosity against outsiders continued. With the discovery of the bodies, evidence that murder had been committed was established; now came the hunt for and arrest of those responsible. Florence told Betty the town's civic leaders were strangely quiet in deploring a crime that was now irrefutable.

A week after the three bodies were found, the Neshoba County fair opened. This greatly anticipated annual event attracted everyone—white, black, and Indian (many Choctaws lived in Neshoba County)—from miles around. Established in 1888, the fair had something for everyone: political speeches, pony rides, good food, lemonade, horse racing, farm and handiwork exhibits, school plays, recitations, and tent shows. One of Betty's favorite excursions was an annual visit to the Neshoba County fair. She went down to visit Flossie for fair week almost every year. That year, she noted the crowds were heavily peppered with the khaki-clad auxiliary policemen, members of an arm of the Klan. Just before dusk on the fair's second night, a low-flying plane dropped leaflets from the White Knights of the Ku Klux Klan of Mississippi, welcoming visitors to the fair. The leaflet consisted largely of an interview with a "Klan officer prepared in the public interest." Some of the questions and answers were:

Q. What is your explanation of why there have been so many National Police Agents involved in the case of the "missing civil-rights workers"?

A. First, I must correct you on your terms. Schwerner, Chaney and Goodman were not civil-rights workers. They [were] Communist Revolutionaries, actively working to undermine and destroy Christian Civilization.

Q. But aren't all citizens, even communists, entitled to equal protection under the law?

A. Certainly. But the communists do not want EQUAL treatment under the law. They want FAVORED treatment under the law.

Q. What persons would have a motive for killing them?

A. There are two groups which could have done it. (1) American patriots who are determined to resist Communism by every available means, and (2) The Communists themselves who will always sacrifice their own members in order to achieve a propaganda victory.

Q. Do the White Knights of the KU KLUX KLAN advocate or engage in unlawful violence?

A. We are absolutely opposed to street riots and public demonstrations of all kinds. Our work is largely educational in nature. We make every effort that sober, responsible, Christian, Americans can make to awaken and persuade atheists and traitors to turn from their un-Godly ways. We are under oath to preserve Christian Civilization at all costs. All of our work is carried on in a dignified and reverent manner. We operate solely from a position of self-defense for our homes, our families, our Nation and Christian Civilization. . . .

Betty and Florence watched the flurry of white drift from the sky, but there was no visible reaction to the leaflets. People stuffed them in their pockets and went on with the festivities, creating an "aura of strange unreality."

The week after the fair closed, COFO's Freedom Summer project ended, and most of the student volunteers from the North headed for home. The report COFO compiled and submitted to the Mississippi Advisory Committee of the Civil Rights Commission confirmed it had been a summer of violence. In addition to the three murdered workers, at least four persons were shot and wounded, fifty-two were beaten or otherwise injured, and about 250 were arrested in connection with the summer project. Thirteen Negro churches were destroyed by fire, seventeen other churches and buildings were damaged by fire or bombs, ten automobiles were damaged or destroyed, and there were seven bombings in which no damage occurred. COFO reported that approximately seventeen thousand black residents of Mississippi had attempted to register to vote. Many were beaten when they tried, and only sixteen hundred of the completed applications were accepted by local registrars. In an effort to address Mississippi's separate and unequal public education system, forty-one "Freedom Schools," attended by more than three thousand young black students, had been established throughout the state.

Betty was told it had been too dangerous until mid-August for COFO workers to go into Neshoba County, but after the bodies were found, COFO designated the county an important location for the continuation of their work. In late August, they leased a building in Independence Quarters, the Negro area of Philadelphia, and a dozen volunteers moved to town. In their efforts to keep the civil rights workers out of Neshoba County, Klansmen became strident. The COFO workers were visited the next night by armed men and told to get out. The COFO workers refused. Later that week, Sheriff Rainey and Deputy Sheriff Price served summonses on the workers to appear in court to answer charges about the validity of their lease, and ordered them out of their headquarters on threat of arrest for trespassing. The civil rights workers did not vacate the building or appear in court.

No further "legal" action was taken, but a nightly Klan parade of cars and pickup trucks circled the COFO office and the surrounding area—as Florence Mars says in *Witness in Philadelphia*, "like a strange funeral procession with guns sticking out of the windows." Having received bomb and burning threats, the civil rights workers posted two observers on the roof every night to watch for bombs. COFO was pledged to non-violence, and the workers were virtually defenseless; however, fully armed Negro men, residents of the area who were not militant but fully prepared to return fire for fire, watched over the COFO workers. The situation was a tinderbox ready to explode. Mars observes, "The only law standing between the Negro community and the Ku Klux Klan was two FBI agents who patrolled the area every night. Local law enforcement took no notice of the night riders." All this was closely watched and reported to the national Civil Rights Commission.

In September, a federal grand jury was convened in Biloxi

to review the situation in Neshoba County, and Florence, known to government agents as a "friendly," honest witness was called to testify. When she returned to Philadelphia, she received phone calls late in the night warning that she would be punished for testifying "against our boys." She was told her barn was to be bombed and burned. The Klan organized a boycott against her stockyard, where she held weekly sales, and rumors spread that she was working for COFO. Frustrated and worried she went to the mayor and talked to several prominent businessmen in her Methodist church. She received sympathy, but no help. The weeks dragged on, with Florence feeling totally alienated from her community. The pressure on her stockyard increased, and by the middle of November, Florence told Betty she would have to sell it. Betty was dismayed. She and Bill had also received nasty, threatening phone calls, but as a white lady married to a Southern planter, she felt safe, never in physical danger. But Florence was intimidated; she sold her business.

On December 4, 1964, the FBI arrested twenty-one men, and Rainey and Price were among them. At the time of the murders there was no federal murder statute, and those arrested were charged with violation of the dead men's civil rights. The men arrested were released on bond, and the town quickly rallied to their support. A defense fund placed collection boxes in most of the local businesses.

The following spring Florence told Betty that things seemed more relaxed in town, and she did not feel as harassed. But it soon became clear that the Klan still wanted to punish Florence. The next summer, when Betty made her annual visit to the Neshoba County fair, she noticed the police auxiliary—the Klan's force—was still very much in evidence. The night after Betty went home to Rainbow, Sheriff Rainey arrested Florence on an ill-defined charge as she was leaving the fair. She spent the night in jail. She told Betty later that, behind bars in a dark, dingy cell, unable to sleep, she paced the cell through the night with the friend who had been arrested with her, and cried. Florence had hit bottom. She was defeated. She had tried to fight the Klan, and she had lost. Her friend said things would look better in the morning. Florence did not believe her, but they did.

Florence's arrest was the beginning of Sheriff Rainey's downfall. When she was released the next morning, her lawyer friend insisted she go back to the fair, where she was met with kindness, sympathy, and support. Rainey had overstepped. He had openly shown that he did not respect or obey the rule of law, but obeyed his own rules. Plus, he had violated a basic tenet of the unwritten Southern code of manhood: He had embarrassed and maltreated a respectable lady. In 1967, the case involving the deaths of the three civil rights workers went to trial in federal court. Rainey was acquitted, but six others, including Price, were convicted. Rainey's term as sheriff ended in November of 1967. After the trial, stigmatized by his role in the events, he was unable to find work and moved out of town.

# A Balancing Act

*The trickiest thing about strength and warmth is that it is very hard to project both at once. This is because strength and warmth are in direct tension with each other.*
    —Johann Wolfgang von Goethe

Betty was torn. As long as she could remember, she had known her life had a purpose: believing that every citizen, regardless of race or color, should be treated equally. During the 1960s her force of character and natural qualities of leadership placed her squarely in the midst of the raging civil rights struggle. It was time to break the mold and rid her homeland of Jim Crow's destructive power. She was not afraid to stand up for what she knew was right. She and John Doar, President Kennedy's lawyer from Washington, frequently argued about how best to integrate Southern culture. Betty believed the first step was to change people's hearts. Doar maintained integration would be accomplished only after the laws were changed.

Viewing Betty Bobo Pearson's life is like looking through a large, brilliant prism. There are so many aspects to her personality, her character, it is difficult to realize they all belong to the same person. In addition to her strong sense of purpose, she has a keen interest in adventure, loves anything that involves challenge, and always makes sure to take others along with her. Good friends tell of her infectious sense of play, her desire for new experiences, and her offbeat ways of having fun. She enthusiastically embraced the Delta culture's tradition of generous, congenial hospitality, while at the same time working to realize the ideal of racial equality. A given day might see her acting as a civil rights activist marching in a protest parade, or submitting a committee report on police brutality in her beloved Delta homeland. That same evening she might welcome guests for a gourmet dinner or informal cook-out in the garden. Puddin remembers the easy familiarity she, along with other workers at Rainbow, enjoyed, helping to host the plantation's many visitors and getting to know them. On other days, Betty volunteered for the literacy program at Parchman prison, or played golf with Bill or tennis with her women friends, or dug in her beloved garden, or supervised the construction of walls and paths from handmade bricks, salvaged from an out-house tumbled by a tornado. Dook Petty, Rainbow's overseer, always asked any man applying to be a tractor driver if he knew how to lay bricks. When the answer was no, Dook said, "You'll learn."

After Frank and Betty Stovall introduced her to fly fishing at their fishing camp on Beulah Lake, Betty, hooked on the new sport, convinced Bill they should create a fishing spot at Rainbow. The Pearsons bulldozed a shallow pond out of one of the swampy sloughs on their property, shaped a low dirt wall around its edge, and built two piers on opposite sides. Always searching for the best before she embarked on a new project, Betty thoroughly researched fishing ponds. Although she knew bream are the most fun to catch, she learned that if a pond is stocked only with bream, the water becomes too crowded for any of the little fish to grow large enough to fight when striking the bait. Putting bass in the pond solves this problem. Bass find baby breams delicious.

The Mississippi Department of Fish and Game stocked the pond with bream and bass. The Pearsons, eager to share the thrill of the catch with others, hosted frequent fishing parties for friends, plus an annual fishing rodeo—a lazy day of hamburgers, hot dogs, cold drinks, and fishing for all the Rainbow workers and their families.

Betty loved to fish alone early in the morning. She took immense pleasure in the quiet solitude as the sun rose over her pond at dawn. One morning, while out alone casting her line, she heard a strange rustling behind her. Investigating, she came face to face with an alligator, eight to ten feet long, wallowing in a shallow, muddy ditch separated from the pond by a dense patch of bushes and reeds. When she was a child, there were alligators everywhere in the Delta, but by the 1960s alligators were rare. She decided to befriend the creature and, from that day on, took it large servings of rancid chicken wings whenever she went fishing. At times—particularly in the spring—when the Pearsons heard the alligator's long, low wail, Bill teased Betty, saying it was a lover's lament for her. Betty said it sounded more like the creature's hunger pangs. Calling on the alligator became an adventure for the many guests at Rainbow, but Betty's friend proved to be shy of strangers and would not always stick its head out from his muddy lair.

Betty had an ecumenical spirit. She grew up in the Methodist church in Clarksdale, attended the Presbyterian church in Sumner with Bill for eight or nine years after Erie was born, and in 1958, the Pearsons helped establish the Episcopal Church of the Advent in Sumner. Bob Bailey, who served as senior warden at the Sumner church in its early years, said, "Once Betty became an Episcopalian she was active in the Church from top to bottom, locally and statewide. She was a sweet, nice person, but she was really strong. One time she chewed me out really good when I wanted to go over budget on some additional pipes for the church organ." Betty knew how to manage money. A doer, generous with her time and her talent, she was the first female senior warden at the church in Sumner, president and chairman of training and development of the Episcopal Women of Mississippi, a member of the executive committee of the diocese, and chairman of the board of trustees at All Saints Episcopal School in Vicksburg. But Betty's thoughts never strayed far from play. Church leaders remember her showing up at important committee meetings in Greenville or Jackson in low golf shoes, sport socks, and casual sports wear, while every one else was wearing business attire.

If there was something that needed to be done, Betty didn't wait for someone else to do it; she stepped forward to make sure it happened. Enthusiastically inclusive, Betty always carried others along with her. One year in the mid-sixties, the women of the Sumner church decided they wanted to create a cookbook. Betty helped gather and select the recipes, typed them up, organized the format of the book, and mimeographed copies for distribution. *The Gravel Road Gourmet*, by the women of the Church of the Advent, was so successful they had to mimeograph a second edition.

Reynolds Chaney, the Episcopal priest in Greenville during the late 1960s, has good memories of Betty:

> She was just fun to be around. She had such vitality.
> Never offensive, Betty had a direct and clear way of saying
> pithy and important things. She was a unique spirit who
> made you feel good, but she could really be wild at times.
> Stubborn, always clear, she had her own opinions and
> couldn't be overrun. Betty affirmed other people. You felt
> better after talking to her. With a twinkle in her eye she

always treated others as equal, even when she disagreed with them. She had a real strong sense of social justice and couldn't be run over, always determined her opinions would be heard. Betty didn't see herself as a savior, just true to her own beliefs—fully alive and full of joy.

Betty's strong convictions made her a driving force. Once involved in a project, she often took over, running things her way in a forceful yet friendly manner. Friends and co-volunteers who did not agree with her plan of action or the timing of a particular project might be firmly chided, but were never rebuffed. She did not hesitate to tell a close compatriot when she thought he or she was wrong, making it clear she "honored you as a person, even when she didn't like the way you thought or acted."

Chaney, who was deeply committed to social justice (he was one of few whites in his town who kept his children in public schools in the 1960s), served with Betty on a number of social justice projects. He said that Betty took him to task one day for not doing more and moving faster to change the racial composition of his church. He explained, "I have a commitment to all the people in my church to be their pastor, not their conscience. I work to enable them to make their own decisions." Chaney respected Betty for the actions she took, even though at the time it was hard to realize much social change. Only later, looking back, was change apparent. Years later, in the mid-1990s, during a dinner party at Frank and Judith Mitchener's, a man Betty first knew when they both attended Clarksdale's all-white segregated grammar school, remarked, "Well Betty, you sure dragged us into the world of integration, screaming and yelling." Pausing for a moment he added, "Well, now it's done, I figure it's okay."

When a group of Betty's friends learned about the Laubach

Method for teaching adults how to read, she went to the superintendent at Parchman prison to ask if they could develop a program for illiterates in the women's camp. This request was made during the one period in the 1960s when the superintendent of the prison was open to having outsiders come in and offer programs for the prisoners. The superintendent agreed, and Betty and her friends found a Laubach Method instructor to train a group of four white and two black women how to teach adults to read. Roy Bascomb, the young priest at the Sumner Episcopal Church agreed, that Betty's group could use the parish hall for training.

Parishioners found out two black women were coming to the church for something other than cleaning, and "a couple of men started raising Hell." Roy called Betty to tell her about the pressure he was under, but told her that he was perfectly willing for them to go on with the program. The decision was up to her. Betty said she thought about it long and hard: "Roy was really a good guy, facing incredible stress." After talking it over with Bill, she went back to Roy, saying, "There has to be a place where we don't back down to societal pressure, and the church is probably the best place to make that stand."

Six women learned the Laubach Method and began teaching the women at Parchman, who were all black. Because the program was voluntary, Betty never knew if there were white women who couldn't read at the prison, or if there was an aversion to—or perhaps a prison policy prohibiting—integrated groups. The inmates had books and lesson plans, but one of the women Betty taught was older and said that the only thing she wanted to read was the Bible. Betty found a child's book of Bible stories, and that's what they used to teach the woman to read. She was so pleased and grateful. Betty said, "It was one of the most rewarding experiences

I've ever had." There were other programs during that period. "They had this good superintendent, who didn't last long." Mike Sturdivant Sr. taught financial fundamentals to a group of men who were about to be released. They learned how to take care of their money, how to use a bank account, how to balance a bank statement, and how to prepare a budget. At the same time, Betty led a group of women ready to be released: "We talked about nutrition, how to plan a balanced meal, how to clean a house, make a bed—really basic stuff."

Parchman had a building on the back side of the prison farm that was used as a motel. Here some prisoners, depending on their behavior and records, were allowed conjugal visits. The superintendent was developing a program to help men adjust to life outside prison after they were released. Betty was asked to facilitate discussion for a small group of men and their wives. She later said,

> What an eye-opener! These people just told it like it was and were brutally honest with one another. When I asked them what was their main worry about going back into the free world, most of the men said they worried about whether or not their wives had been true to them sexually. The women said, although they had missed their husbands, they liked being in control of their own lives and were worried that their husbands would come back and completely take over. There were just a lot of basic relationship problems these people were willing to talk about very openly, as opposed to my experience with church groups, where people tried to be open but still very polite.

None of these programs lasted long. The superintendent who initiated and supported programs taught by outsiders left. Betty recalled, "A new, hard-nosed guy was appointed and they closed all of the volunteer sponsored programs. The only people allowed in after that were ministers."

Closer to home, Betty's innate curiosity took her on a new adventure. Edwin "Bunny" Mullins, her oldest friend, whom she'd known all of her life, introduced her to a new experience. Bunny had grown-up in Clarksdale, graduated from Cornell with a degree in architecture, practiced in California, and moved back to Clarksdale to farm his family's land. He planted two or three marijuana plants in his backyard, but hacked them down when they grew above the cypress fence surrounding his property. The local police had arrested someone for growing the weed, and he was afraid that someone would see his plants and report him. After drying the leaves in his attic, he phoned Bill and Betty to say, "The marijuana is ready." One afternoon a few days later, Bunny appeared at Rainbow with roll-your-own cigarette paper and crushed marijuana ready to smoke. Bill and Bunny lit up, but Betty, who had quit smoking years before, "didn't want to choke." Bunny said she could also eat marijuana, so Betty, who had made brownies that day, sprinkled some marijuana on top of one, and ate it. "I probably put on too much marijuana, I don't know . . . but I had a very bad trip." After Bunny left, Bill and Betty went to bed.

He was asleep and I woke him up and said, "Bill I have something to tell you. I do not want you to be upset, but I do want you to know it." And, he was saying, "Uh-huh, what . . . what do you want to tell me?" And, I said, "Well, I'm going to die. I can feel the blood in my veins getting slower, and slower, and slower, and as soon as it stops moving, I will die. But I don't want you to worry about it because I'm all right about it, you know we've had a happy life, so I don't want to upset you, but I just want you to know that's going to happen." I was just calm as a cucumber, so he puts his arms around me, and pats me, and says, "Well, OK, Babe, thanks for telling me" and went back to sleep. And I went to sleep in his arms and woke up the next morning feeling fine.

Ingesting pot did not become part of Betty's life. If she were going to "travel," she wanted fun and excitement.

Jean and John T. Fisher, a generation younger than the Pearsons, were by the early 1960s a part of Betty and Bill's extended family. John T's sister was married to Oscar Carr, Betty's life-long friend and compatriot in the civil rights struggle. Although the Fishers lived in Memphis, much of their social life revolved around the activities of family and friends in the Delta. Ardent supporters of the civil rights movement, they were frequent guests at Rainbow, and traveling companions on many of Betty and Bill's weekend outings. Betty's love for thinking big and seeking challenging adventure resonated with John T.

During one winter weekend at Rainbow, Betty suggested the four of them should hike the Appalachian Trail—all 2,184 miles from Georgia to Maine—in increments of three or four days over the next couple of years. That summer they launched her plan at Springer Mountain, Georgia, the start of an initial four-day, three-night trek. Betty had done no mountain training, but she was confident she was in great shape, as she jogged several miles a day and played golf and a lot of tennis. In anticipation of their outstanding adventure, she loaded her backpack with sixty pounds of good-living, including a whole round of edam cheese, a canned ham, and two pairs of new blue jeans, along with other "necessities."

The books Betty read described the route as a "crest trail," and she envisioned enjoying marvelous long vistas while strolling a trail atop the range of venerable mountains. The reality proved to be vastly different. Betty remembered, "It was a long struggle up the trail until you get to the top. You have about three steps along the crest and then you go down again. It was up and down, up and down, up and down, the whole way." Lean-tos, where hikers slept, were placed along the trail, so there was no need to carry a tent. By the time Betty, Bill, Jean, and John T got to the lean-to where they were to spend their first night, Betty had tossed the ham, the cheese, and all other weighty food in her backpack into the woods for bears to find. When dinnertime came, "All we had to eat was that horrible freeze-dried stuff that is not really food." When they departed the next morning, Betty left behind her two pairs of brand new blue jeans "in case someone else who came along might want them."

At the end of the second day, after hours of arduous hiking, the Pearsons and the Fishers came upon a cold mountain stream at the bottom of a hill below the lean-to where they planned to sleep that night. Off came their shoes and socks and the four bone-weary hikers plunged their aching feet into the icy water—pure bliss. When Jean, John T, and Bill were ready to hike up to the lean-to, Betty lingered. Thirty minutes later, she finally pulled her feet out of the stream and put on her shoes, socks, and backpack for the final trudge. Betty could not take the first step. Totally fatigued, her leg muscles refused to respond. It was impossible for her to lift her foot. She shuffled to the side of the steep trail steps leading up to the lean-to, fell to her knees, grabbed hold of the nearest bush, and pulled herself up, crawling bush-by-bush up the hill to another freeze-dried dinner.

The lean-to was full of hikers that night, and every one of the more than dozen bunks—packed tight against each other, jammed with sleeping bags—was occupied. As soon as Betty finished what she insisted was "erroneously called dinner," she crawled into her sleeping bag and immediately fell asleep. In the middle of the night a low, rumbling roar awakened her, and thinking it was Bill snoring, she nudged him. Bill turned over and woke, but the snoring continued. "It was the man on my other side, who I didn't know. I certainly couldn't wake him up," Betty said. There was no more sleep for her that night. In the morning it was pouring down rain, and when she learned one of the hikers was leaving the trail that day, Betty begged a ride into town. His car was parked at a takeout spot directly down the hill from the lean-to. Jean said, "If you're going, I'm going, too." Betty and Jean spent the next night in a motel. Betty never again mentioned a desire to hike the Appalachian Trail.

In the next few years, frequent canoe trips on the rivers in the Arkansas Ozarks—the Eleven Point, the Spring, and the Buffalo—satisfied her yearning for good exercise and wilderness ventures. She found small streams that fed the larger rivers where she gathered fresh, pungent watercress for the tastiest of salads. Away from civilization and light pollution, Betty said, "It was thrilling, once the sun had set, to watch satellites [a new phenomenon of the modern world] fly through the deep, dark night sky among the brilliant, diamond-like stars."

In 1968, Betty hired Mr. Goldman, a local carpenter, to build a guest wing on their house, using old cypress wood salvaged from the tenant shacks torn down when new houses were built for the workers at Rainbow. The edges of the beautifully weathered boards were rough and uneven, presenting a problem for creating the paneling she envisioned. She asked Mr. Goldman to make a forty-five degree angle cut on the edge of each piece. He shook his head. "Ah, Mrs. Pearson, you don't have to use rotten wood. I can get you some new, smooth boards at a reasonable price." Betty demurred, and he again resisted when—not wanting to have molding at the ceiling—she ordered a precise, clean cut at the top of each board, adding "Take your time, be careful, I know you can do it." Several weeks later Mr. Goldman appeared at the front door with three friends, saying, "I'd like to show my friends the beautiful rooms we created."

Two years later Betty called Mr. Goldman when the Pearsons decided to enlarge Bill's bathroom and add an exercise room and sun deck. He responded. "Ah, Mrs. Pearson, I really liked working for you, but I can't." Stunned, Betty asked, "Why?"

"My wife told me if I worked again for 'them Nigger lovers,' she would leave me."

Betty greatly admired Fannie Lou Hamer, the forceful spokesperson and leader in the struggle for civil rights in Mississippi. A destitute former field worker, Hamer was twice denied the right to register to vote, and arrested, jailed, and beaten with other Negroes attempting to be served at a public lunch counter. In 1962, she was finally allowed to register, but was unable to vote. She had not paid the poll tax for the previous two years.

Hamer tried to work within the regular Mississippi Democratic Party, but she was locked out of party meetings. Along with others, she concluded the only way to oppose the segregated Mississippi political machine was to establish the Mississippi Freedom Democratic Party (MFDP), a racially integrated Democratic party. When the 1964 national Democratic convention was held in Atlantic City, New Jersey, the regular Mississippi Democratic Party sent an all-white delegation. The MFDP, with sixty thousand members, selected a delegation of sixty-four blacks and four whites. Aaron Henry was elected chair, and Fannie Lou Hamer was elected vice chair. In an effort to be seated as Mississippi's legal and rightful delegation, the MFDP mounted massive demonstrations and pursued political bargaining, resulting in a "compromise." Two at-large seats at the convention were offered to the MFDP, but rejected. Hamer explained, "We didn't come all this way for no two seats." While the MFDP was not seated at the 1964 Democratic convention, their efforts were not in vain. Four years later, the 1968 Democratic Party convention denied credentials to the all-white Mississippi Democratic Party delegation and seated an integrated slate of challengers, the newly formed Mississippi Loyal Democrats. Bill Pearson, Oscar Carr, and his brother, Andy Carr, were members of that delegation.

Betty had been elected as a delegate for this new integrated party, and its leaders begged her to go to Chicago. Believing her participation would break her father's heart, she asked Bill to go in her stead. Bill did and later said, "Senator Eastland never spoke to me again. The only time he saw me, he turned away."

# The Seventies and Eighties

*Full participation in all things is the surest way to happiness, vitality, success.*
—Anonymous

*There was nothing good and decent in this town that Betty wasn't involved in.*
—Bob Bailey

By 1970, violent opposition to integration began to disappear, and the attitudes of white Southerners toward desegregation gradually began to change. There was still resistance, but it was not confrontational. Betty recalls that in the 1960s, when federal laws first ended racial segregation in all facilities that served the general public, her father refused to enter a restaurant serving Negroes. Ten years later, he reluctantly accepted the change, and ate in a favorite lunch spot that served both blacks and whites. Her good friend John Doar was right: Integration might never have happened if they waited for people's hearts to change. Changing the laws had to come first.

Robert Grayson, whose aunt was Bill's aunt's cook, grew up at Rainbow. Robert, his mother, his aunt, and his two brothers lived in one of the houses on the plantation. He moved there when he was seven years old, a year before Bill and Betty arrived. When Erie was born three years later, Robert felt like a big brother to her. He watched her grow up, and he looked after her as any big brother would.

One Sunday morning when he was in high school, Robert's good friend William and another boy came by his place, wanting Robert to go down to Greer's ditch for a swim. Robert told them, "Naw." They shouldn't be swimming in that ditch, and he didn't want to go. They left without him. A few hours later, he and his mother were sitting on the porch, when a neighbor lady drove up with the news, "William got drowned. They haven't yet found his body. Come on, you can ride with me down to where they're looking for it."

When Robert arrived at the bayou where they said William went in, he saw a big man was in the water searching for the body. The man said he thought he felt something soft with his hand and dove under again. William's body surfaced, and the man caught it around the waist. Two other guys splashed into the water, grabbed the body under the arms, pulled it out, and carried it up to the house. Reliving the memory, Robert slowly shook his head back and forth. "Really got to me. It took something out of me. Really had a bad impact. William couldn't be gone, but he was. The drowning hit everyone hard," Robert said. "It took a lot out of Miss Betty, too. She made the ditch off-limits for swimming. Fishing was OK, but absolutely no going in the water—few if any of the black children knew that swimming wasn't like walking, it didn't come naturally. You had to learn certain techniques before going into water over your head. I never learned how to swim."

Betty always wanted a swimming pool at Rainbow. It would be a place for children to learn to swim. Over the years she badgered Bill with that and many additional reasons. A pool would be a welcoming enticement for family and friends, added ambience for their many gatherings in the garden, an excellent source of exercise, and a refreshing respite from the sweltering summer heat. Bill listened, agreed with Betty's points, and said, "Maybe next year." Pools were expensive. That year arrived in the mid-seventies. Bickie and Mike McDonnell were among the dinner guests at Rainbow one night when Betty mentioned how much she wanted a swimming pool. Bill looked up from carving the roast and said "Well, why don't we build one?" Bickie said the next morning, as she sat on the terrace drinking a cup of coffee, a steam shovel arrived to begin digging a huge hole in the Pearson's backyard. Once she got her okay, Betty wasted no time. Betty's pool took almost thirty years to materialize, but when it was built, every black child on Rainbow—plus all the other black children in the area—were invited to learn to swim in the Pearson's pool. Betty hired a talented college student to give weekly swimming lessons to these children.

Robert Grayson said, "I'll tell you one thing, Miss Betty is definitely a nice lady, she will definitely help you any way she can." His grandchildren learned to swim in the Pearson's pool. He didn't trust the water, but he remembers his younger brother and Erie had such fun swimming in "Miss Betty's pool" right after it was built—even though integrated swimming would have alarmed many of the townspeople.

Betty's own words, found in *Pieces from the Past* by Joan H. Sadoff, tell the poignant tale of her daughter's wedding.

In 1972, our daughter, Erie, who had graduated from Swarthmore College, married Michael Vitiello, a boy from New Jersey, whom she met in college. Erie had always wanted to be married at home so we planned a garden wedding at Rainbow. My parents weren't sure about their granddaughter marrying a Yankee, but they rallied and said that they, with my brother and his wife, would host the rehearsal dinner night before the wedding. Then Erie told us that Michael's sister was married to a black man. When we told my parents, they were stunned and said they couldn't possibly have the rehearsal dinner because of "what people would think." If we went on with a home wedding, where would this couple stay? I said, "With us, of course," and told them that while they were welcome to be a part of the celebration, all of Michael's family would be there and were welcome. Andy and Oscar Carr and their wives, old friends from Clarksdale, hosted the rehearsal dinner in Susie and Andy's home, and other friends, Jane and Wes Watkins from Greenville, had a dinner party the night before. The wedding was a smashing success. Many of Erie and Mike's college friends came down for a week of parties, picnics and softball games. Our close friends, while perhaps not agreeing with us about mixed marriages, were constant in their love, and put on a wonderful wedding luncheon for 200 or so guests.

My parents attended the wedding. At one point in the afternoon, I saw my father in conversation with Erie's black brother-in-law. When they left, I walked them to their car and told my father how glad I was they had come. I said, "I know this hasn't been easy for you and that you're here because you love Erie and me. Thanks for being nice to Mel." Tears rolled down his cheeks.

Although there were undercurrents of tension, Erie and Michael's wedding presented Rainbow Plantation at its best. It was a wonder-weaving, welcoming celebration on a beautiful June afternoon, in a beautiful garden for so many people: close, life-long friends, Erie's first cousins on both sides, civil rights workers, everyone who worked at Rainbow, Bill's book club, and friends and acquaintances of all ages and persuasions. There were a few notables like Scott Peck, the psychiatrist and bestselling author of *The Road Less Traveled*, and John Doar, the lawyer from the Justice Department who was a key figure in the civil rights struggle in Mississippi during the 1960s, and who was awarded a national Medal of Freedom in 2012.

Betty said, "The core of the wedding was a week-long house party. Ten or twelve friends of Erie and Michael from Swarthmore came down to Mississippi for the big event. We had just finished building new houses for the tractor drivers, and one of the houses had not yet been moved into, so we set it up as a dorm, with the girls downstairs and the boys upstairs." Since everyone always talked about the "church family," the Pearsons invited all the members of their church in Sumner, around one hundred people. Some of the church invitees didn't respond or come, but Betty was impressed that Mrs. Yandell—a woman who was part of Betty's mother's generation and who shared her mother's beliefs about race—called to say, "she would not come to the wedding, but she wanted me to know she appreciated being invited."

On the big day, Erie wore a simple white Mexican wedding dress at the mid-day ceremony, and five of Betty's close friends (Tonya Marley, Margaret Henderson, Gwin Buford, Barbara Mullins, and Jane Graham) prepared luncheon for the two hundred guests. A fancy chicken breast entrée, green salad, asparagus casserole, mixed fresh fruit, and wedding cake were served from a long buffet table out on the terrace. White, linen-covered tables and chairs were set up under the pine trees for the adult guests. Small individual picnic baskets containing fried chicken had been prepared for the children, who ate on Mexican serapes spread out under the pecan trees. Betty recalled, "How great it was to see the children of the folks who lived and worked on Rainbow, playing with the children of the other guests—black and white boys and girls having such a good time together."

Wine, iced down in big washtubs dotting the garden, was poured by four Rainbow tractor drivers for whom Betty had bought black pants and white shirts. When Betty went into the kitchen around five that afternoon to check on dinner plans, one of the tractor drivers was leaning against the counter. Betty said, "Claudie Boyd, you're drunk!" He replied with the sweetest smile, "Sho is, but ain't it been a beautiful day!"

Puddin said that earlier that day Betty sent Charlie, one of the men who worked at Rainbow, into Webb for ice. The man selling the ice would not give it to Charlie; he had heard that a black man was staying at the Pearsons and wanted to see for himself. Puddin said, "When that ice man arrived at Rainbow, Miss Betty, realizing why he'd not given the ice to Charlie, put her hands on her hips, and told him to take his ice right back to his own freezer. She didn't want it." Betty then phoned her brother Bob in Clarksdale, asked him to buy ice, and sent Charlie to Clarksdale to pick it up.

Erie and Michael had planned to leave for Philadelphia that evening, but they were having such a good time, they told Betty they were staying another night. Betty acted quickly. She had not anticipated that the bride and groom would spend their first night together at Rainbow: "Erie's bedroom was right next to Bill's and mine. I got Louise and Mel, Michael's sister and her husband, who were staying in the guest room at the other end of the house, to move to Erie's room, and free up the guest room for Erie and Michael." She then rushed into the kitchen to pull out of the freezer the four big lobster casseroles she'd made a couple of weeks before. "Bill had fussed at me, asking why in the world I was making so much food. I must have had a premonition—thirty to forty folks stayed for dinner"—and the party lasted well into the night.

Betty was a paying patient at the Tutwiler Clinic, about a ten-minute drive from Sumner, where 72 percent of the patients, unable to pay, received free medical care. The clinic was built in 1964 and was funded by the Rural Health Initiative. When that federal program closed in 1981, the building was donated to the town of Tutwiler. In 1983, Sisters of the Holy Names, led by a physician, Sister Anne Brooks, DO, approached the town council, and were allowed to re-open the clinic as a full-time outpatient facility.

When Betty learned the children who came to the clinic had no place to swim, she said, "Bring them to Rainbow." The nuns rounded up the children for an afternoon at the Pearsons' beautiful, shady swimming pool, where Betty fed them homemade peach ice cream. Sister Anne remembered, "The peach ice cream Puddin probably made was the crowning glory. The kids had so much fun. But that was Betty. Everybody is welcome. Everybody is special. Everybody gets the best, no matter your age, social standing, or color of your skin." Anne Brooks said, "Betty was a wonderful mentor. She was like part of our Tutwiler family [of five nuns]. A wonderful example of what we all would like to be. The way Betty and Bill treated their people was a model."

Starting in the 1960s, Betty experienced great support from people in the Episcopal Diocesan and National Church. She became involved at every level of the Episcopal organization. The little church in Sumner was a great training ground for young priests, and she was a great trainer. When Henry Hudson, who had been working at a "high church" in another town, arrived at the Church of the Advent, he introduced himself as Father Hudson. Betty, knowing pretension would be resented in Sumner, quickly said, "Forget that. You're Henry here." Father Henry Hudson went on to bigger things. He became rector of Trinity Church in New Orleans, and he continued to appreciate his early tutelage from Betty. Many of the priests that served in the small Sumner parish, or who worked with Betty in some capacity within the church, went on to responsible positions of leadership in the Episcopal Church at both the state and national level. Betty was elected president of the Mississippi Episcopal Church Women, served as a delegate to the 1973 Church Women's National Triennial convention, and was a member of the Mississippi Diocesan Committee. After serving for six years on the board of trustees of All Saints' Episcopal School in Vicksburg, she was the first woman in the school's sixty-nine-year history to be elected chairman of the board. The previous year, Bill Pearson had been the first layperson in the school's history to serve as chairman of the board.

Jack Allen, originally from Helena, Arkansas, became the presiding bishop of the United States. He and Betty worked closely together when he was the head of All Saints School, and later when he was bishop of Mississippi. Allen recognized Betty's unique leadership qualities and called on her skill to help parishes and conventions throughout the state and nation sort through thorny issues. She had been an eager participant in the church-sponsored, T-group training designed to help people become sensitive to body language, and learn to listen to what others were saying and give feedback without demolishing or running over others' feelings. Always curious and eager to learn new ways of doing things—be it for effective leadership or successful gardening—Betty was intrigued with the process and enjoyed employing these new techniques. She was asked to meet with church vestries to help them determine their church's future.

By the 1980s, federal laws designed to end racial segregation and protect civil rights and equal opportunity for all United States citizens were in place. In 1983, Martin Luther King Jr., the martyred leader of the civil rights movement, was memorialized. Dr. King's birthday, January 15, was declared a federal holiday to give national recognition to the heroic effort and sacrifice of all those who had devoted their lives to changing the conscience of their nation. Increasing numbers of volunteer programs and community action groups were organized to improve the living conditions, education, and economic plight of Negroes (now referred to as African Americans), trapped by past injustice.

A few years after Habitat for Humanity International was founded in 1976, the young Methodist minister in Sumner invited the group's founder, Millard Fuller, to a meeting in the basement of the Sumner Presbyterian church. When Fuller explained the mission of the nonprofit, ecumenical Christian ministry—which involved volunteers building houses with donated supplies for people in need—he received an enthusiastic response. A group in Sumner organized the Mississippi Delta Habitat for Humanity, the first Habitat chapter in the state. The Presbyterian, Episcopalian, and Methodist ministers, along with Annie Laurie "Dink" Morrow and Betty, who became the first secretary, were the driving force. Delta Habitat purchased two lots in the town of Webb, then selected two families (one black, one white), to be the first recipients of Habitat houses. The group had money in the bank to pay for pouring the slabs and beginning construction, but their efforts were blocked.

Not every heart in the Delta had changed. A petition opposing the proposed construction was circulated and signed by a majority of the people in Webb, and the Webb town board repeatedly refused to grant building permits for the two houses. Although lawyers advised the Habitat board to go to court, the board felt that if the houses were built under court order, the fundamental purpose of Habitat would be lost. Its purpose was two-fold: to build decent houses for people who have no other way to finance them, and to solicit broad community support for these projects. The committee believed even though the permits to build could be granted, Habitat's desire for community support would be defeated by any court action.

Stymied, but not willing to give up, Betty sought a way to break the impasse. She knew that Jimmy Carter and his wife, Rosalynn, actively supported Habitat for Humanity International, and she wrote the former President.

September 14, 1985
The Honorable Jimmy Carter
Plains, Georgia 31780

Dear President Carter:

The Board of Mississippi Delta Habitat has been told that you are aware of the situation in Webb, which we understand has the dubious distinction of being the only community ever to deny a building permit to Habitat, and I am writing for your advice and help.

Enclosed is a brief description [summarized above] of the

situation which I wrote [about] a couple of weeks ago at the request of some of the people in my church. The only sentence I would perhaps change is the one that says "no one in Webb—would be against Habitat if they understood the true facts of the Habitat program and purpose." That may not be 100% accurate!

The situation began with one individual, who unfortunately is very wealthy and therefore powerful, who circulated a petition against Habitat, and worked on the fears of many of the white people in these small Delta towns, by telling them that Habitat's purpose was to move enough black people into the town so that they (the blacks) could gain political control of the town. Something like 90% of the whites in Webb signed the petition (including the local Baptist minister) and also many blacks, who were easily intimidated. The Town Board took this as a mandate, and by now has stood by this position so long (we have requested the permits three or four times), that there is no graceful way for them to back down. As I explain in the enclosure, we are pretty sure we could get the permits by going to court, but feel that this might defeat our ultimate purpose, although it is a constant temptation, at least with me, to want to beat them at whatever cost.

One of the dynamics of this thing that you and Mrs. Carter will perhaps understand, is that the center of the opposition to Habitat has been in the Southern Baptist Church in Webb. This is primarily true because the man who circulated the petition is a Baptist, and controls the church by being such a large contributor that the church depends on him to pay the bills. However, it has also been true that in all of these little towns, the white Baptist congregations hardly ever join in any local ecumenical projects or programs.

I realize that you probably still have almost as many demands on your time as you did when you were in the White House, and I'm sure people are constantly asking you to come somewhere to do something. But I also know that you are a committed Christian and a staunch supporter of Habitat, so I am going to respectfully ask that you and Mrs. Carter consider paying a visit to Webb, for the purpose of meeting and talking to some of the people in the community who might be persuaded to support our efforts. To be perfectly honest, I have no idea if such a visit would do a lot of good, or if it would simply make the opposition more defensive, but I hardly see how things could be any worse than they are now.

My husband, Bill, and I live in the country about two miles from Webb, and we would be extremely honored to have you and Mrs. Carter as our guests. I don't know what security measures are necessary for the travels of a former President, but if it would be advisable, Bill and I could simply move out, and turn our home over to you and your party.

I hope that it will be possible for you to come to Webb, but in the event that you can't do that, we would greatly appreciate any comments or advice that you and Mrs. Carter could give us on constructively dealing with this impasse.

Sincerely yours,
Betty Pearson, Secretary
Mississippi Delta Habitat for Humanity

Jimmy Carter did not come to Webb. However, when the problem in Webb reached a stalemate, Frank Mitchener donated property adjacent to the Tutwiler clinic to Delta Habitat, and the board decided to sidestep the Webb controversy. The first Habitat house in Mississippi was built in Tutwiler. Ora Johnson was the first Habitat resident in Mississippi. By 2014, with effective encouragement from the sisters at the Tutwiler clinic and a dedicated board of directors, thirty-five Habitat houses had been built in Tutwiler.

# Meeting Mother Again and Again and Again

*Families are forever, and he wondered if the slogan was meant as a promise or a threat.*
　—Brady Udall

*Children betrayed their parents by becoming their own people.*
　—Leslye Walton

Although issues surrounding race had fractured Betty and her father's relationship, Bob Bobo loved his daughter, and their basic loyalty to each other was never in question. Betty's parents made their inheritance plans, deciding who would get what when they died. Father would leave the house and land at Bobo to Bob; mother would leave her land at Farrell to Betty. Betty and her brother, Bob, would inherit the house in Clarksdale jointly. The insurance business would be left to Bob, but he would pay Betty for her share.

In 1974, two years after Erie's wedding, Betty's mother spent most of the summer in Memphis in the Baptist Memorial Hospital owing to metastatic breast cancer. The cancer had spread to her bones, and she was receiving treatment to manage the pain. Betty's father did not want her to be alone, so for almost two months, Betty drove to Memphis every Monday morning and stayed with her mother until Friday. Betty's father worked all week in Clarksdale and drove up on the weekends to be with his wife. Betty was grateful for this time with her mother. They had never really bonded. Mother and daughter were so temperamentally different, but when her mother died—with Betty holding her hand—Betty felt the barrier between them had been demolished. Betty's words, written in a letter sent to Jean Fisher and other close friends shortly after her mother's death, captured her mood.

The bad times bring out either the very best or the very worst in us, and in my mother's case, this painful illness summoned the best. She met the pain, the lack of privacy, the gradual physical deterioration, with unfailing courage, grace, and consideration for others. I learned a lot about how to live from watching her die.

The relationship between parent and child is always ambiguous . . . dependence/the need to be independent; love/hate; belonging to one another/yet needing to be separate. My mother was a possessive woman, and so for me the struggle to establish my own life style was so difficult that I guarded against too much closeness. I'm grateful that these last two months gave us the opportunity to close the circle, to experience once again our mutual love and need, to learn together that love so easily survives conflicts in ideas and life styles. In too many relationships I've had to say, "I wish I'd said . . ." or "I wish I'd done . . ." before it was too late. But this time we hung in there together and I have no regrets. I'm sure she had none, either. That's a good feeling.

Intimately sharing someone's death, especially over a period of time, is both a privilege and a threatening experience. My mother shared with me her feelings about dying, her fears, her sorrow over leaving my father, and also her deep faith. In order to be with her in a supportive way during that time, I had to face honestly my own fears and uncertainties about death, and that meant becoming vulnerable in a way that was and is frightening. I suppose it is the first time in my life I've ever tried to be totally open, and it was rewarding and enriching, but it has also made the pain more difficult to handle—my defenses still aren't properly in place. So I've learned something about the value both of necessary defenses, and of allowing oneself to be vulnerable.

There were times, especially early on, when I could do things to help: talk to doctors, get better nurses, arrange for special food, protect the patient from the system. Gradually, though, the feeling of being able to do something was replaced by the frustration of being utterly helpless to do *anything* in the face of this relentless disease, culminating in the last 24 hours when even my physical presence was of no importance to her, and only filled my own need to be with her when she died. For me, that knowledge of my existential helplessness is the most frightening thing about the confrontation with death. It has taught me something about my own deep need to control events, to manage, like the child whistling in the dark, the need to control here and now is a defense against the admission of ultimate helplessness.

I envy those of you who are sure there is a God, and even who He is. My only claim to faith is that I will be faithful in spite of my doubts. And yet, at the worst of times I was somehow in touch with a constant deep source of strength that seemed transcendent to me, that I cannot name with any certainty, but which I trust.

I'm grateful for some things I learned, or relearned, or learned at a deeper level, about human relationships. First, how much I depend on Bill and how much strength he gives me. I could be supportive of Mother and Dad only because he was always there behind me, like a strong, solid wall—no way for me to fall.

Second, the tribal quality of a family, especially a large family, and how comforting that can be. Brothers and sisters, cousins, aunts and uncles, grandchildren, all drew the wagons up in a circle around my father, and the unselfish outpouring of love and comfort and support was something to see. When the chips are down, friend, nothing takes the place of the clan.

And finally, and the reason I'm sharing these meandering thoughts with you, how very aware I've been this summer of what Duncan Gray calls one's "personal church," the small group of people whose love has strengthened and sustained me. I've realized, not only how important that community is to me, but also the rather astonishing fact that because we already had a relationship of trust and love, I didn't always need your physical presence or your conscious support. Some of you I have been in touch with and your expressions of concern and love have meant more than I can ever tell you. But those of you who didn't know where I was this summer, with whom there has been no communication these past few months, were just as surely a source of support. I learned that just knowing that I have a "personal church," and that you would be there if I needed you, was enough—true communion is not a sometime thing, and I didn't have to talk to you to feel your presence. . . .

About two weeks after Lenora died, Betty was settling back into the daily routines of country living, when her father arrived out at Rainbow. He greeted her with a firm hug, and before sitting down, he tossed some papers on the coffee table saying, "Here is a copy of your mother's will." Since Betty thought she knew everything that was in it, she didn't bother to pick it up until after her father left. But later, when she read what her mother had stipulated, she could not believe her eyes. "I was absolutely stunned to learn that she had left her land at Farrell to [Betty's brother] Bob, with the provision that he pay me some dollar amount. . . . I don't remember how much. I have never felt so totally rejected and unloved in my life. I couldn't stop crying. It was several days before I could pull myself together enough to drive to Clarksdale to talk to Dad about it, and then I couldn't talk . . . I was crying so hard." Throughout that past summer, during the many hours, the many days, she had spent with her mother, there had been no mention of a change in Lenora's will.

Betty's father said that he had begged Lenora not to do it. But because Betty and Bill were so deeply involved in the civil rights cause, and Erie had a black brother-in-law, she had become obsessed with her heritage—"paranoid" about the possibility that a black person would some day own her land. Both of Lenora's parents died before she was ten years old, and the land she inherited was all she had left of them. Was this a way for Lenora to honor and protect her parents' legacy, as well as her own beliefs?

Lenora's will provided, however, that her husband, Robert E. Bobo, had a life estate in whatever she, the deceased, had owned. The land at Farrell belonged to Betty's father until his death. He was adamantly opposed to what Lenora had done, and he said if Bob agreed, he was going to reinstate Betty's inheritance. Bob agreed. When their father died in 1979, Betty inherited the Farrell land.

Betty was deeply upset and confused. She had opened her heart to her mother, and for the first time in her life she felt an honest bond between them. She had shared and tried to absorb her mother's pain, shared her mother's death, and thought hard about her own life. She had been forced to face and relinquish some of her own need to monitor and control her emotions—but now this. Through it all, her mother knew she had disinherited her and never mentioned it. How could it be? But feeling that life was for the living, Betty—well-practiced in controlling her emotions—pushed these questions deep into the recesses of her psyche and worked hard to focus on the joy, the fun, and the service that gave purpose to her life.

Now in her mid-fifties, Betty was increasingly involved with her church work, Episcopal consultancies, All Saints School, prison programs, T-groups, entertaining, tennis, golf, gardening, and beautifying. She and Bill had trees planted around their church and along the main streets of Sumner. They traveled to Europe. They traveled to Mexico. Once, when the Pearsons were on a trip to Spain with their friends the Mullinses, Betty and Barbara spent an afternoon at the beauty parlor. Disgusted with the time spent having her hair shampooed and set after after having spent "all this money to get to Spain to see the sites," Betty took a pair of cuticle scissors from her bag and whacked off her hair. Inch-long locks could be washed in the shower. She would waste no more time in beauty parlors.

Life felt abundant. Things were going well, until a strange uncertainty began to gnaw at Betty's exuberance, her unbounded curiosity, her joy in life. It was the mid-1980s, a few years after her sixtieth birthday, when Betty's enthusiasm for her many projects and her delight in the company of others slackened. She found committee work a burden, and she resigned from several local boards. Not wanting to give in completely to this increasing apathy, she maintained a few of her consultancies within the church at the diocesan level. She labored to keep up a pleasant front, even as she felt her inner self crumbling. At night, plagued by an inexplicable, growing despair, she found it hard to sleep. Bill worried. Erie worried.

Erie, now living in New Orleans, called her mother at least twice a week begging, "Please, Mama, please find someone to help you. You're not yourself." She told her mother about a good therapist in New Orleans, saying, "You could rent an apartment close to us. Please, Mama, you've got to do something." Betty, who had always met life and crisis straight on with self discipline and a strong will, felt she was coming unglued. As long as she could remember, she felt her life had a purpose. No more. Life felt meaningless. Never before had she felt such uncertainty. Erie was right. She should do something. She couldn't go on like this. A professional therapist might be able to help. Even a change of scene might help. With a resolve honed through years of purposeful living, Betty pulled herself together, went to New Orleans, rented a condo, and met Beth Breese, the therapist Erie recommended. She liked Beth. They were about the same age, and from their first meeting, Beth seemed more like a good friend than a therapist. They agreed to meet for an hour session three mornings a week.

The change felt good. Living in a city had its charms, and it was a new experience, distracting and different. Her grandchildren, James and Elizabeth, stayed with her almost every Saturday night, and on Sunday mornings, the three of them headed to the flea market to search the stalls for Star Wars characters the children didn't have. Betty remembers, "The French Quarter was magical, like a European city, everyone strolling the streets, an old man selling balloons, magicians, jugglers, acrobats performing." Often when the children stayed with Betty, they took the streetcar to Windsor Court, the luxury hotel on Gravier Street, for Sunday afternoon high tea. The outing was "a very high treat for ten-year-old James who took everything, especially the hot chocolate and dessert tray, very seriously."

However, after six weeks in New Orleans, Betty harbored doubts that the therapy sessions were worth the time and money. She was sixty-five years old—maybe too old for therapy. She liked Beth, but she'd had experienced no startling breakthroughs of self-understanding in talking with the therapist. These weeks in New Orleans began to feel like an extended vacation. This was all about to change. In hindsight, Betty realized it must have taken six weeks for her to build up enough trust—or become so completely frustrated with their lack of progress—to finally take a risk.

At the Monday session of the seventh week, Betty let down her reserve enough to tell Beth the terrible feelings she had, "the sort of things you'd never, ever think of sharing with anyone." She was sure that Beth would be repulsed and reject her, or at least think less of her. Looking back, Betty realized that she'd taken the first step in breaking down an inner dam of resistance she'd hidden from everyone all of her life. It was the beginning of a dramatic change in the way Betty would eventually understand herself and her relationship with others. On the following Wednesday, "almost too scared to go to my session, I couldn't believe it, when Beth greeted me, as always, warm and friendly, with not the slightest hint of censure."

With near total recall, Betty described what happened next. After she entered the office and lowered herself into a comfortable chair, she waited, not knowing what to say. Beth took her time, paused for a few moments, looked directly at Betty, and asked, "Well, how's it going, any new thoughts?" Nothing had changed in Beth's open, accepting manner, but Betty froze. "My mind blocked. I could think of nothing to say." Beth, unperturbed, didn't prompt or push. She let the hour pass in "superficial, meaningless chit chat." "After the session ended, I was truly puzzled. This made no sense," Betty said. On Monday, she had braved an incredible hurdle, lowered her guard, talked about the emotional chasm, the ambivalence, she'd always felt towards her mother, and her despair over their relationship. She had shared forbidden feelings, feelings she had never before shared with anyone, not even Bill. But "Beth listened calmly with no comment, not asking a single question." Betty thought once she finally pried open the tight seal on those putrid emotions, she would be ready to dig deeper and get to the bottom of her misery, purge the poison that was eating her alive. Instead her tongue tied, and Beth offered no help. The covering on Betty's buried shame slammed back and shut tight. She could just as easily have been at a Delta cocktail party for the rest of their hour together. She could not fathom what was going on.

Before her session on Friday, Betty concluded she must not be a good candidate for therapy. When they met, she told Beth she felt completely blocked. Beth nodded and looked directly at her: "You took some risks with me on Monday. You became more open to me. Our relationship became deeper and more intimate. Why do you think you blocked right after that?" Bewildered, Betty responded, "I don't know." Beth told her to try to get in touch with her feelings. Betty tried. She shut her eyes and opened them again, thinking hard, looking down at her feet. "Then I clasped my hands tightly in my lap, and felt a cold, creeping deadening in my chest—no coherent thoughts, I felt only raw fear. I was afraid, terribly afraid, but afraid of what?" She remembered that every nerve inside her body tightened. She felt out of control, panicked, unable to speak. As if coming through a deep fog, Beth's voice said, "Betty, for some reason you are afraid of intimacy. We are going to have to keep working on that."

Over the weekend Betty had so much to think about, and she was relieved to be by herself. Erie and Michael took the children to the beach, and Bill, who usually drove down from Rainbow on Fridays, phoned the night before to say his aunt needed him in Sumner. When Monday came, Betty was ready to talk. She had one big question: "I know I need to be in control. I'm so afraid of rejection and I have a hard time sharing deep feelings, but none of this seems to me to explain the kind of terror I felt on Friday. I was really scared. It was so intense." Betty paused and swallowed hard. "It felt like something much deeper, more basic." Before answering, Beth let out a long, deep breath. "I think you are right, Betty. It reminds me of the kind of stark terror that you see in children who were abandoned in infancy and are always in terror that it will happen again." With Beth's words, Betty burst into tears, sobbing. Beth handed her a box of tissues, gently rubbed her hunched shoulders, and waited. After five minutes—which seemed like an hour—Betty wiped her eyes. "I wasn't abandoned, I was thrown away," she concluded.

In the coming months, Beth helped Betty get in touch with feelings she never before had allowed to surface. It was not easy. She was afraid of intimacy. She felt thrown away not once, but twice. First, she was thrown out of a car window when she was eighteen months old. Less than a year later, her bed was moved downstairs away from her mother after the birth of her little brother. Why had her mother rejected her? Was Betty's strong need for control a defense against hurt?

After three months, Betty gave up the rented condo and returned to Rainbow, but she still had a lot of work to do in therapy. Over the next year, she drove the three hundred miles to New Orleans every week, and stayed two or three days in a room she rented from Erie's next-door neighbor in Old Metairie. During those visits, Betty met twice each week with Beth, and attended a therapy group with five or six of Beth patients. Betty had been in therapy for almost a year when she was diagnosed with breast cancer and went to the M. D. Anderson clinic in Houston for surgery. Betty's surgeon arranged to have the six weeks of follow-up radiation done at the Ochsner Clinic in New Orleans, so that Betty could continue her regular sessions with Beth and her therapy group.

The five or six women in the therapy group bonded and became very close. Wanting to add to the conviviality of their meetings, Betty began to bring popcorn. When Beth heard about the popcorn she immediately told Betty, "This must stop. You are not to play hostess, this is not a party. You are here to explore your feelings, not entertain your guests." That was the end of the popcorn. Betty realized, "I put a lot of miles on my car during those six years, but it unlocked so many things that have made all of our lives happier."

Betty came to understand how difficult it had been for her mother, who was driving when the train crashed into their car, killing her father-in-law and severely injuring her mother-in-law.

How deeply this must have affected my mother. She must

have been very depressed after the accident and felt a lot of guilt. Maybe Mother felt I blamed her for what happened. I don't know. When baby Bob was born the next March, she had an innocent baby, who was hers to love without complications, while I represented a past history of regret. I always felt there was some sort of thing between Bob and my mother I couldn't break into. I used to fantasize that they had some kind of secret language, and if I could just catch onto what it was, I would be okay.

Betty never felt close to her mother: "I never had the kind of relationship a little girl ought to have with a mother. But I don't think my mother, nor I, as I grew up, understood how the emotional toll we each suffered [from the accident] shaped our relationship. It was one of those impossible situations that happen and you never get over it." Betty lamented that things might have been different if therapeutic intervention had been developed when she was a child, and its value for dealing with such trauma understood.

She received a great deal of security and love from others.

I adored my Daddy, always felt a part of his life and his mother, Big Mama, was absolutely my idol. I adored her and was convinced that she loved me more than any other grandchild. If she didn't, it didn't make any difference, 'cause that's what I believed. She was a wonderful person and I spent a lot of my childhood with her, following her around in the garden and doing things with her. It wasn't until I was grown and had my own house and garden that I realized how much tension my mother was under. She raised her family in my grandmother's house. It was my grandmother's garden and my grandmother's servants.

My mother did not have her own home until she moved to Clarksdale when I was in college.

Betty's grandmother was a very strong person, accustomed to running her own house. The house was one she and her husband built in 1918, after the original 1880 Bobo plantation house burned to the ground. After the train wreck, when she finally got home from the hospital, her grandmother—then in her early forties—regained her strength and took charge of her household. Adjusting to her life without her husband, she poured most of her affection into little Betty. Betty came to the stark realization that her mother had always lived in her mother-in-law's domain, but her grandmother was good to her mother in many ways. Her mother told her, "You know, Sis" (Sis is what her mother called Betty), "Big Mama was the perfect mother-in-law. If your father and I had an argument, she always took my side. She never, ever agreed with Robert if he and I were in disagreement."

Having made profound breakthroughs in self-understanding and gained a new perspective on her past, Betty's life began to purr back into its normal rhythm. She and Beth, who lived in Abita Springs in a lovely old cottage with a big garden, became good friends and occasionally shopped for plants or had dinner together. While alone in New Orleans, Betty spent most of her free time building an enormous Victorian-style doll house, which she placed on a rotating platform. Back home, this creation became a major source of enchantment for the children of friends and neighbors Betty invited out to Rainbow. There had always been baskets of toys and games for these young visitors, who claimed Betty as their "fairy godmother," but the doll house was special. It was fully furnished, down to a beautiful miniature dining room table with a full set of tiny china plates, and a refrigerator with a plastic turkey. The hardwood floors were covered with needlepoint rugs, the first made by a loving friend and sent to Betty when she was in the hospital in Houston.

Once again captivated by the magic of Rainbow, Betty felt renewed, enthusiastic for the activities she enjoyed, and filled with love for the people she cherished. She was happy to be home. With Beth's help, she had purged most of the demons that had driven her into a period of despair, not realizing that another self-defining moment was about to surface. One night after Bill had gone to bed, Betty was out in the sunroom by the pool, sitting on the couch reading. Then, she recalled, "The strangest thing happened. I felt something hard pressing against my back. I was totally panicked. This was the only panic attack I've had in my life. My mind was not on any of the stuff I'd been through in therapy the months before, and I didn't know what was happening. I felt as if I was being pressed against something really hard. Like metal or a brick wall or something. I started breathing hard—panicky. I was absolutely scared to death. I thought, what is happening to me? Am I having a heart attack?"

It was almost eleven at night, but Betty called Beth. "Beth, if I've waked you up, I'm sorry, but I've got to talk with you." Telling Beth how she felt, Betty said, "I'm absolutely scared to death, and I don't know why. I'm just terrified. I've never been this frightened before in my life." Beth said, "I think you are reliving the moment you were thrown out of the car in front of that train." Betty said, "I was only 18 months old." Beth said, "I don't care. You can still have reactions to something that traumatic in your life, particularly if it was physical. You don't really remember it, so you can't intellectualize the event, but you are re-experiencing those physical feelings you had." As Beth talked, Betty started breathing better and calming down. She was opening the final, intricate fold of the origami of her emotional life. Her heart, her soul, the very core of her feelings lay exposed. In cellular memory, one holistic theory holds, everything we experience from the moment of conception is imprinted in our cells and constitutes a collective energy field, which operates behind our subconscious mind.

Betty did not remember the wreck, but from the stories she had heard all her life, it was not hard to reconstruct what happened. She was sitting on her grandmother's lap—a secure cocoon of love since the day she was born—listening to nursery rhymes, when she heard a clickety-clack outside their car. Wanting to see what it was, she scooted toward the new sound. There was an ear-splitting crash, and

> I felt myself thrown from the car and slammed down on something hard. It really hurt and no one could hear my screams over the roar of the huge, hissing monster carrying me along. When the monster slowed and chugged to a stop, I was flung away. This time I hit the ground and my mouth filled with dirt. Everything hurt. Strange arms picked me up and carried me to my mama. But Mama was screaming. Why was Mama screaming? I'd never known my mother to scream. Always before when I fell down, she was the first person to run to pick me up and cover me with kisses. Now she was screaming. There was chaos and sirens, confusion everywhere. Why had Mama thrown me away?

Over the coming year, Beth helped Betty come to understand that beyond the reach of her conscious knowledge, the train wreck loomed large in her psychic memory. Beth told her that after such a major trauma any young child would need her mother to be there night and day. But when she was taken to the hospital and placed in a body cast with her arms extending over her head, Betty was besieged by strange, unfamiliar people and surroundings. Her mother, her grandmother, every important person in her life had vanished. Back home at Bobo, when her mother reappeared, Betty felt rejected because Lenora was depressed and gave the new baby most of her attention. When her grandmother came home from the hospital, Betty was again surrounded and supported by her grandmother's all-encompassing love, a love directed solely at her.

Understanding how that terrible trauma had affected everyone in her family for years, Betty felt a new freedom, grateful she no longer had to deny and bury her negative feelings, her self-recriminations, her fear of intimacy, and her fear of rejection. This understanding brought new meaning and a different understanding to words from so long ago: "Betty, God reached down and plucked you from in front of that train because He has something very special he wants you to do with your life."

# Leaving Rainbow

*Somewhere over the rainbow*
*Skies are blue*
*And the dreams that you dare to dream really*
*do come true.*
  —Yip Harburg

In 1993, the Pearsons, both in their seventy-first year, sold Rainbow. Betty said, "Rainbow will always spell 'home' for me, it nearly broke my heart." She adjusted.

After they moved into Sumner, into a small house on a small lot facing the Cassidy Bayou and near old friends, Betty continued to host her "magical" dinner parties, participate in church and community betterment projects, promote racial reconciliation, and garden. Bill missed his office in their house at Rainbow, so Betty talked to the new owners, and receiving their permission, had Bill's office sawed off their old house in the country, hauled into town, and attached to their new house. The size of their yard in town was like a postage stamp compared to the land Betty had gardened in the country, but to the delight of neighbors and friends who enjoyed the bounty from her green thumb, she found a solution. She tore up the driveway for her tomatoes, built a greenhouse, and planted every inch of available soil with a sampling of the multitude of vegetables, fruits, and flowers she had cultivated at Rainbow. Puddin continued to make her famous relish from Jerusalem artichokes grown in Betty's new garden.

Betty spent hours almost every day digging, planting, weeding, pruning, and picking—closely trailed by Larry Heard, her right-hand man in the garden, who caught her if she started to fall. Betty's passion for her garden never diminished, though she increasingly experienced bouts of vertigo as she entered her eighth decade. Her neighbor Carolyn Webb saw how Betty "banged herself up and bled profusely" when she fell, and worried because Betty refused to wear gloves or cover her arms while gardening. A lymph node had been removed during Betty's operation for cancer in 1988, and as a result the slightest scratch often caused massive swelling and infection. Physical challenges and various operations for internal repairs, like every problem Betty had ever faced, slowed her down for a spell, but never stopped her.

The Pearsons loved to entertain. Betty said, "Bill always said we ran a hotel, and it's true. We had many overnight guests, singly and in groups—friends from Mexico, Canada, England, India, Bill's book club, my therapy group, and in the sixties civil rights workers, lawyers, writers, reporters. Puddin loved having company . . . she was the queen bee." Believing life is a gift, Betty wanted to share its abundant riches. Good friends remember that when she entertained she created magic—memorable, unique, fun, sometimes over-the-top happenings. The Pearsons' sacahuil (tamale) festival in 2001 vividly illustrates Betty's approach to entertaining. This was their second sacahuil festival. The first was held at Rainbow in 1983. In 2001, wanting to liven-up their annual Fourth of July party, Bill and Betty decided to throw another one. Betty commissioned the construction of a huge metal cooker, like one they saw in Mexico when visiting their friends Buford and Malvina Anderson. Betty contacted Diana Kennedy, the author who piqued Bill's interest in the sacahuil years before. Kennedy was on a book tour in the US and replied, accepting the invitation to attend the party and participate in cooking a four-foot tamale for over forty guests.

This sacahuil fiesta, another carefully planned and executed bacchanal gathering, was not only covered by Michael Donahue for the *Memphis Commercial Appeal*, but was featured in *Saveur* magazine in an article by Mary Ann Eagle, who described the "cheerful fractiousness that came over the trio of cooks, Buford Anderson, Betty Pearson and Diana Kennedy as they prepared their sacahuil." Eagle reported, "Betty laughing said, 'I told Diana at one point, do you think that writing five Mexican cookbooks makes you more of an authority on Mexican cooking than Buford and me?'" Abby Taylor, a friend and helper at the party said, "Ms. Pearson and Ms. Kennedy both thought they were admirals." It was another one of Betty's memorable parties. A decade after she and Bill moved to California, friends in Memphis and the Delta still talked about the 2001 sacahuil fiesta in Sumner.

It is hard to imagine any place in the world where there is greater celebration of traditional holidays than in the Mississippi Delta, and the fireworks over Cassidy Bayou on Christmas Eve ranks as one of the region's most celebrated traditions. Every year on the night before Christmas, from seven o'clock until eight o'clock in the evening, the winter sky over Sumner filled with brilliant explosions and wondrous patterns of luminous color. The grand finale of the pyrotechnics, a high cascade of star-like sparkle falling into the water of the bayou below, is followed by a cacophony of honking horns, as spectators from miles around load into cars, and head for church, home, or the after-fireworks party that used to be at Bob Bailey's. More recently, they have gathered in the Murphys' front yard around a big bonfire.

Until 2004, on the next night—after the children hung their stockings, Santa paid his visit, and families exchanged gifts and ate their midday Christmas dinners—there was another celebration: the Pearsons' annual Christmas night party, a tradition with a modest beginning that grew into a huge, much anticipated, celebration. In the early years the party was a small gathering of a few close friends: the Bufords, the Mullinses, the Marleys, and the Mitcheners. They came by Rainbow on Christmas night for a peaceful, relaxed drink, quiet conversation, and a song or two around the piano. There was no food, unless someone went to the kitchen to make a turkey sandwich. After Bill and Betty went to Spain in 1971, they began to make a big pot of turnip greens soup for the group on Christmas night. During the next few years, the party grew, and so did the selection of food. In addition to the turnip greens soup (now a Christmas night tradition), there was a Jezebel ham, which Frank Mitchener always insisted on carving, T. C. Buford's smoked salmon, and a caramel cake from Calhoun City. Mike Wagner attended his first Christmas night party in 1986, and remembered thinking, "Why in the world would that lady be serving turnip greens soup at what surely was bound to be a nice party."

After the Pearsons moved to Sumner in 1993, the party expanded, adding new neighbors, married children, and their children. Caviar and champagne became the fare, along with the turnip greens soup. Mike Wagner said, "By 2004, that party rocked. Harvey [Henderson] always carnivorously scooped most of the caviar off of the top of the cream cheese before most of the company arrived."

Betty was eighty-four when the Emmett Till Memorial Commission was established in Sumner by the Tallahatchie County Board of Supervisors in 2006. The commission was formed largely through the efforts of Jerome Little, one of the first blacks to be elected—in 1996—to the Tallahatchie County Board of Supervisors. In 2006, he became the board's president. The commission's stated purpose was to foster racial harmony, restore the Tallahatchie County Court House, the site of the 1955 Till trial, and to preserve and teach the history of the civil rights movement in the area. During the first few months of the commission's existence little happened. There were nine members, six black and three white. The black members feared if there were a white majority, they would take over, run things, and exploit the memory of Emmett Till to encourage tourism. Jerome Little, who worried that the initiative would falter, contacted Susan Glisson, the executive director of the William Winter Institute. The institute had been founded several years before by the former governor of Mississippi to promote racial reconciliation in his state. Glisson stepped in to help, saying Governor Winter told her, "If the Commission was going to succeed, it needed Betty Pearson as a member. She's about the only person with the trust of both blacks and whites."

Betty said, "I didn't even know I was on it [the commission] until they had several meetings, and then one day I just happened to bump into Jerome [Little] and he asked why I hadn't been coming to the meetings. He said that the board had appointed me when they established the commission, but, if that was true, no one had bothered to tell me." Soon after Betty started attending meetings, the board voted to have an equal number of black and white members and to have co-chairs, one black, one white. Betty Pearson and

Robert Grayson (who grew up at Rainbow) were elected co-chairs. Betty understood the black members concerns, and she listened. As trust grew, she begged the members to call her by her first name. Willie Williams, a black minister and auto repair shop owner was the treasurer. Betty asked him one day, "Willie, do you think you could find it within you to call me Betty?" He replied, "No Ma'am, I can't do that."

On the morning of October 2, 2007, four hundred people gathered in front of the Sumner courthouse to witness the commission's historic commemoration of Emmett Till. The Winter Institute Newsletter reported:

One of the highlights of the event was when the Emmett Till Memorial co-chairs—Betty Pearson, a white woman, who attended every day of the 1955 trial, and Robert Grayson, the first African American mayor of Tutwiler, [who was fourteen at the time of Emmett Till's death, the same age as the murdered boy]—took turns reading the statement of regret signed by commission members:

We the citizens of Tallahatchie County realize that the Emmett Till case was a terrible miscarriage of justice. We state candidly and with deep regret the failure to effectively pursue justice. We wish to say to the family of Emmett Till that we are profoundly sorry for what was done in this community to your loved one.

At the close of the ceremony, a newly installed historic marker, the first permanent memorial of Till's tragic death, was unveiled.

In 2008, Betty and then Bill were hospitalized, and their daughter, Erie, made two trips to Sumner, in as many months from Davis, California, where she, Michael, and their children, Elizabeth and James, lived. It was then that Bill and Betty decided it was time to pull up their deeply entrenched roots in Delta land, and move cross-country to the University Retirement Community (URC) in Davis, four blocks from Erie and her family.

When the Pearsons packed up for California, there were heavy hearts in Sumner. Puddin, who had been with them for over fifty years, asked Betty, "What am I supposed to do?" Betty responded, "Puddin, you've done your work . . . you're done with your job." Puddin retired to the house in Webb the Pearsons had purchased for her. Bill advised one of his tractor drivers, Larry Heard, not to take the first job offer he would receive: "They are going to go as low as they can and you can make them go as high as they can, because they know you are good."

It did not take long for Betty to become a vital part of her new community. One of the residents said, "Betty just seems to draw people to her and carry them along." Within three years she was elected president of the URC resident council. Another resident remarked that Betty was "the best leader we've ever had." As president, Betty served as a non-voting member of the URC board of directors. At the end of her term as president, she was asked to be the first voting resident director on URC's board. In October 2013, Betty Bobo Pearson received the Jane Pomeroy Award, an honor given annually by the URC council in recognition of outstanding service. Two years later, in the same month as her ninety-third birthday, Betty Pearson—still showing her stuff as a remarkable leader—was the recipient of the Leading Age California Resident of the Year Award.

On October 12, 2013, during halftime at the Rebels versus Texas A&M game, in the Vaught-Hemingway football stadium at Ole Miss, the William Winter Institute announced the establishment of another annual award: The Florence Mars and Betty Pearson Community Leader Award. In presenting the award to Dick Molpus, the award's first recipient, Reuben Anderson, the first African American justice to sit on the Mississippi Supreme Court, said, "It is only appropriate to present Dick with an award named after Florence Mars and Betty Pearson, both of whose humble convictions inspired loyalty and quietly brought about results."

# Betty Bobo Pearson's Guiding Principles

- You are here for a purpose.
- Life is a gift.
- Everyone counts—all people need a chance.
- Don't be afraid to break the mold.
- When you find a heart-mate, appreciate it all the way.
- Always search for the best.
- If you see something that needs fixing—fix it.
- Don't be afraid to take charge—lead/help others better themselves.
- Open your heart and give time to those who are hurting and searching—but hold your own ground so they may find their own direction.
- Find joy and spread it—create an open, hospitable, fun world where all feel welcome.
- Learn to live with pain—don't let it stop you.
- Know yourself—at some point turn inward, find your true core.
- Reflect—hold onto the good, let the rest go.
- Forgive those who have hurt you.
- Be grateful for the good in your life.

# Acknowledgments

The inspiration and the genesis of this book are found in the heart and mind of Jean Fisher, who one afternoon said, "You should write a book about Betty Pearson." I asked, "Who is Betty Pearson?" Jean answered, "The most remarkable woman I have ever known." After watching videos about Betty's involvement in the civil rights movement, driving to Clarksdale to talk with her brother Bob Bobo and his wife, E'Lane, who generously pulled out the family picture albums and scrapbooks, Jean and I flew from Memphis to California so that I would meet Betty, her husband, Bill, and their daughter, Erie. I agreed that Betty Bobo Pearson is indeed a very remarkable woman, someone whose story is an inspiration to others, and Jean Fisher shepherded me through the whole project.

In capturing Betty's story we have many people to thank. Judith and Frank Mitchener not only hosted our several stays in Sumner and introduced us to the key people we wanted to interview, they also provided outstanding historical background about life in the Delta and key influences on Betty's world. Alma Puddin Tucker, Andy and Suzy Carr, Robert Grayson, Susan Glisson, Luther Brown, Lee Aylward, Sister Anne Brooks, Carolyn Webb, Bob Bailey, Lee McCarty, Curtis Wilkie, Daney Kepple, Bickie McDonell, and Reynolds Cheney all had stories to tell. During the course of the research, other impressions of Betty's personality emerged from casual conversations with her numerous friends. Jim Lanier's contacts in the world of Southern historians, Susan Cushman's in the world of local writers, and the Clarksdale and University of Mississippi librarians were most helpful.

The encouragement and advice of Leila Salisbury, director of the University Press of Mississippi, plus the readings and editorial recommendations of Norma Watkins, Ellen Prewitt, Leslie Van Gelder, and Mary Anne Eagle were invaluable, as were the day-to-day interest, support, and critiques from my husband and first reader, John.

ACKNOWLEDGMENTS

# Works Consulted

## Newspaper and Periodical Archives
*Clarksdale Press Register*
*Denver Post* (pictorial)
*Floridian Times Union*
*Jackson, Mississippi, Clarion-Ledger*
*Look* magazine
*Life* magazine
*Memphis Commercial Appeal*
*New Orleans Times-Picayune*
*New York Post*
*New York Times*
*Newsweek* magazine
*Saveur* magazine

## Publications and Records
1939 Clarksdale High School annual
1943 University of Mississippi annual
*Cotton Grower*, January 1984
*Delta Magazine*, "Stopped in Its Tracks," May 12, 2002
Episcopal Church of the Advent, administrative records
*Humane Medicine: A Journal of the Art and Science of Medicine*, Canadian Medical Association, October 1991

## Selected Books
*Clarksdale and Coahoma County*, Linton Weeks
*David L. Jordan: From the Mississippi Cotton Fields to the State Senate, A Memoir*, David L. Jordan with Robert Jenkins

*Dixie: A Personal Odyssey Through Events That Shaped the Modern South*, Curtis Wilkie

*The Mind of the South*, W. J. Cash

*The Past That Would Not Die*, Walter Lord

*Pieces from the Past*, ed. Joan H. Sadoff

*Rising Tide*, John M. Barry

*River of Dark Dreams*, Walter Johnson

*The Strange Career of Jim Crow*, C. Vann Woodward

*Witness in Philadelphia: A Mississippi WASP'S Account of Civil Rights Murders*, Florence Mars

*Womenfolks: Growing Up Down South*, Shirley Abbott

### Videos

Betty Pearson, Tape 1 & 2, William Winter Institute for Racial Reconciliation

Delta State Center for Culture and Learning—Oral Histories

Standing on My Sisters' Shoulders (youtube.com)

### Selected Internet Resources

American Experience—The Murder of Emmett Till, People & Events, PBS

Civil Rights Movement—Black History, history.com

Civil Rights Timeline, infoplease.com

History of the Women Marines, womenmarines.org

Women in Military Service for America, womensmemorial .org

# Index

Parchman prison, 133, 137–38
Pearson, Erie. *See* Vitiello, Erie
Pearson
Pearson, William Wallace (Bill,
Betty's husband): agricultural
innovation, 80–81; Cotton
Grower Achievement Award,
82; discharge from Army Air
Corps and return to Delta,
69–70; Harvard University
Advance Management
Program, 86; marriage to
Betty Bobo, 69–76; Rainbow
Seminars, 82
Peck, Scott, 149
Pettey, Dook, 80, 133
Philadelphia, MS, 11, 118
*Pieces from the Past* (Sadoff),
38, 98, 147
Popham, John (Johnny), 16
Power, Tyrone, 56
President's Committee, 98,
Presley, Mary Martha, 69
Price, Cecil, 120

Quantico, VA, 54

Rainbow Plantation: Betty as
mistress, 82–83; Betty making the crop, 86; fishing pond,
133–34; gardens and land-
scaping, 100–103; improve-
ment of tenant housing, 85;

remodeling of house, 99–100;
swimming pool, 103, 147
Rainey, Sheriff Lawrence A.,
122, 124, 129, 130, 131
Ralston, Frank, 36
Rollins, Rosie, 86–89
Rosedale, MS, 69
Rosenthal Competition, 44

sacahuil festival, 175–76
Sadoff, Joan, 38, 147
sailing, 33–34
Schlei, Norbert, 106
Schwerner, Michael, 96, 120,
123, 124, 126, 127
sharecroppers, 14
Simms, Bobbie, 87
Simpson, William Marion, 79
Sitton, Claude, 122, 123
Slayden, Phil, 124
Smith, Robert B., III, 16
Spendrup, Ellen (Aunt Ellen),
123–24
Steak House Café, 125
Strider, Sheriff Clarence, 14–16
Strong, Virginia (Ginny), 63, 65
Student Nonviolent
Coordinating Committee
(SNCC), 103
Sturdivant, Mike, Sr., 138
Sumner, MS, 70, 92; Christmas
Eve, 176; Pearsons' move to,
103